Doctrine and

Vol. 42   May / June 199

Abortion, Law and Conscience

DOCTRINE AND LIFE is published ten times yearly. It appears monthly, except for the May-June and July-August issues. ISSN 0012-466X

Subscription rates
To the Republic of Ireland: IR£21.35; *Northern Ireland:* Stg£18.20
To Great Britain: Stg£18.80
Overseas, surface mail: Stg£20.50, US$33.21, Cdn$37.52
Airmail: Stg£29.30, US$47.46, Cdn$53.61

Business address (for business enquiries, subscriptions and advertisements, etc.): Manager, Dominican Publications, 42 Parnell Square, Dublin 1. Telephone: 721611; Fax 731760; [Codes: *National* 01; *From the U.K.* 0001; *International* +353-1].

Editor: Bernard Treacy, O.P., Dominican Publications, 42 Parnell Square, Dublin 1 (for editorial enquiries, typescripts, etc.).

Back issues of DOCTRINE AND LIFE are available on microfilm from: Xerox University Microfilms, 300 North Zeeb Road, Ann Arbor, Michigan 48106, U.S.A.

Published by Dominican Publications, and printed in the Republic of Ireland by the Leinster Leader Ltd, Naas, Co. Kildare.

ISBN 1-871552-29-X

The price of this special issue is £5.99
but those who have entered pre-paid subscriptions
will receive it as part of their subscription
and at no extra cost.

Contents

Introduction *Bernard Treacy, O.P.*	229
Moral Debate and Social Change *Ricca Edmondson*	233
The Conscience of the Voter and Law-maker *Patrick Hannon*	244
Abortion and the Law *Gerry Whyte*	253
European Dimensions of the Abortion Debate *William Robinson*	273
Abortion Law: the Tragic Choices *Simon Lee*	282
Vatican II Perspectives *Louis McRedmond*	298
What Is Christian Teaching on Abortion *David Smith, M.S.C.*	305
Laylines *Seán Mac Réamoinn*	318

DOCUMENTS

Yes to Life *Bishops of Ireland*	326
Abortion and the Right to Life *Archbishops of Great Britain*	336
The Sacredness of Human Life *Irish Catholic Bishops' Conference*	345
Reaction to the Supreme Court Judgement *Standing Committee of the General Synod of the Church of Ireland*	346

Introduction

BERNARD TREACY, O.P.

The debate on the questions raised by the Supreme Court judgement in *Attorney General -v- X. and Others* becomes more complicated by the day, and already there are unhappy signs that we may be facing into a dialogue of the deaf. The labels 'pro-life' and 'pro-choice' are being applied as if they were mutually exclusive badges of dishonour. There have been commentators who suggested that a committed Catholic should not be considered eligible for public office. As if in parody of such penal law attitudes, there have been voices claiming that Catholic legislators with a Catholic conscience are obliged to incorporate Catholic moral teaching into civil law.

The essays which make up this special issue of DOCTRINE & LIFE are offered in the belief that it is no service to truth or charity to reduce complicated questions to simple slogans. Taken together, they try to face up to the unexamined assumptions surrounding the question, Is a Christian law-maker obliged to insert Christian moral teaching into civil law? (In posing this question, it must be remembered that, when it comes to a referendum, every voter is a law-maker.)

The question of whether to enforce moral values by means of legal norms is usually answered by reference to the common good, with the plea that it may, regrettably, be necessary, to restrict personal freedom for the sake of the general well-being of society. This principle is not as helpful as it might appear: both Professor Hannon and Mr McRedmond show that securing and upholding the freedom of the individual is itself part of the common good.

Another well-trodden way of approaching the dilemma is to argue that changing the law will 'open the flood-gates' to wrong-doing. Ms Edmondson's analysis suggests that this argument is not as persuasive as it might appear – it is not at all clear that a legal system is an accurate expression of the norms by which people actually shape their lives.

The question is not, and never has been, whether Ireland should have a law on abortion – a complete ban is itself an abortion-law. The question which surfaced to be decided by the Supreme Court was, What kind of abortion law does Ireland now have? The answer given by the Court surprised many – and angered others. Before deciding whether one approves of the decision, it is necessary to have a detailed understanding of what the Court actually held. This is what Mr Whyte provides. On the question of time-limits, one of the most controverted points, he points out that it is a fallacy 'to assume that silence on the matter of time-limits imply that no time-limits exist at all', and goes on: 'the Constitution does not preclude the introduction of time-limits restricting the availability of abortion.' Because the Court saw a need to introduce greater clarity by means of ordinary legislation, Professor Lee sets out suggestions on what might be taken into account when framing a workable law on abortion, also analysing the British and Northern Irish experience.

Since Ireland joined the European community in 1973, there has had to be an European dimension to Irish law. This is the aspect of the question which Mr Robinson explores, showing that decisions of the European Courts (the Court of Human Rights and the Court of the Communities) are developing a jurisprudence which amounts to an unwritten constitution protecting fundamental rights and freedoms. He questions whether 'the adoption of the Protocol and Solemn Declaration *can* derogate from such a fundamental element of the Community constitution.'

The moral teaching of the Churches, including the Catholic Church, is much more nuanced on abortion than many commentators allow, as Fr Smith shows and as can also be seen in the documents section. To translate such ethical concepts directly into legal norms is not at all simple. What Catholic moral theology regards as forbidden is direct abortion. But it allows that an operation to save the life of, say, a pregnant woman suffering cancer is permissible because what is intended is the healing of the cancer and the death of the fetus, inevitable though this be. Such thinking is not easily adapted to the intellectual ethos of the civil law where a person is presumed to intend the foreseeable consequences of one's actions.

The final section of this issue contains a set of Church documents, showing the range of official reactions to the moral and legal questions surrounding abortion. These include reactions to the Supreme Court decision, but also documents from earlier debates, including the 1980 document from the Catholic Archbishops of Britain to which Professor Lee refers on p. 297.

This work focuses on the legal and political questions which flow from the decision in *X*, Mr Robinson and Mr Whyte showing between them how complex are the legal questions raised when the Supreme Court decision is placed in the context of the rapidly developing legal mechanisms for bringing about a European Union. If only because of the legal complexities, there is a clear need for the debate to be conducted in an atmosphere of paying serious attention to the wisdom to be heard from all voices. It will be important to recognise, with Ms Edmondson, that we must 'attend to the practical details of social contexts' within which people come to hold the views they do.

In this regard, what Ms Edmondson has to say about the position of women and the pressures on many women's lives can be instructive.

A tendency to opt for abortion should not be disconnected from other aspects of women's situation: for example, the fact that it is hard for women to achieve social respect or to fulfil their own capacities at the same time as having children.

DOCTRINE & LIFE will return to this topic in our September issue.

When all the debates have died down, much will remain to be done to deal with the web of social and economic pressures under which women might make the agonised that abortion is preferable to parenthood. Law will have a role to play then, too, in helping to create a society in which women's dignity is more clearly recognised, but law will not be the only means of bringing that about.

ERRATUM On p. 230 the second half of the fourth sentence in the third paragraph should read: '... because what is intended is the healing of the cancer and not the death of the fetus, inevitable though this be.'

Moral Debate and Social Change

RICCA EDMONDSON

In the current debate about abortion law, it often appears that the different speakers inhabit hermetically sealed worlds of reasoning. Trying to understand some of these different worlds, I want to suggest a method of seeing debates themselves as events in society, to be understood more fully in relation to their respective social contexts. This approach does not entail relativism or abandoning commitment; instead, it offers a prospect for some advance in communication. The questions at stake here are too complex to supply us with any simple set of expectations, such as the 'domino theory' of abortion laws; this means that debate between the different positions cannot be settled neatly, and merits examination in itself.

MORALITY AND LAW: AN INDIRECT RELATIONSHIP

The twentieth century has witnessed massive attempts, all over the world, to reconstruct public values via large-scale social and legal engineering – promoting Communism, equality in educational opportunity, Gaelicisation ... None of these attempts has achieved striking permanent success: for good or ill, altering laws does not have a predictable impact on people's views.

Nor, conversely, can a country's values be simply 'read off' from its legal system. Legal provisions evolve from a patchwork of long-drawn-out interactions: struggles for power and influence, tradition, borrowing, attempts to institutionalise social attitudes, as well as sincere efforts to work out the answers to difficult practical questions. Legal structures are not, therefore, phenomena peculiar to themselves, but are the products of processes so varied that they may or may not express what the majority of people in a society really believe.

Nonetheless, since legal regulations are the results of social processes, it would be surprising if we could not tell anything about a society from its legal system. We do learn something, even if it is not quite clear what, about the moral conventions of a civilisation from the laws it tolerates. Laws which, say, allow massive corporate fraud to result in little lasting restraint on its perpetrators tell us something about society though they would not correspond to most people's ethical views.

It is not absolutely impossible to make an impact on legal proposals, as is shown by the example of Fr Peter McVerry and the campaign against the expansion of gaming halls. But, under present political conditions, for individuals to organise social movements for or against particular legal arrangements is hugely burdensome. That's why campaigners tend to be only those who are, for particular reasons, the most committed in each case. The fact that most people tolerate the existence of most laws does not, then, license us to infer that these laws reflect their personal moral views.

It can be difficult even to imagine the effects on society of large-scale legal structures – except, it seems, on questions of religious and reproductive morality. One reason for this exception must be that there is already an established discourse available within which to conceptualise the effect of possible changes. The nature of this discourse frames debate in a particular way. It appears to be comparatively hospitable to the views of people who see legal methods as appropriate for rendering complex shades of moral reasoning.

There is a less developed battery of concepts available to those who see the law as doing no more than lay down a framework for what will be punished and what permitted, leaving moral details to be decided in context. Some analysts argue that women, on the whole, more often fit into the latter category: that they prefer treating cases with complex reference to circumstances, rather than searching for across-the-board solutions to moral questions. To people with this point of view, morally sensitive behaviour can best be encouraged by institutions which develop responsible participation in public life. But such innovative arrangements are currently difficult even to imagine, much less to talk about and campaign for.

All the same, Western legal systems are capable of generating some laws which positively affect morally relevant behaviour – though not necessarily in the expected way, and not necessarily by themselves. Germany, for example, offers financial incentives for protecting the environment by sorting household waste, and to a great extent individuals appear to have internalised this habit. Yet it would be premature to conclude that laws alone have had this result – we need to know more about the forces supporting the trend of this legislation, and the social contexts concerned. If, as is often argued, the Dutch abortion rate is unusually low despite 'liberal' abortion laws, we need to investigate in detail what, in the relevant social settings, makes this possible. If in many social circumstances changes in abortion laws tend to lead, at least at first, to more abortions, this is not merely because values have changed in direct response to legal changes. Even before the legal change there were people who wanted abortions, and now they can obtain them without being punished.

It is hard to see that altering one law could straightforwardly affect some corresponding single 'value', particularly a value of special social significance. Values are not single, isolated phenomena which can be detected by a single method, such as asking people or observing their daily conduct. Rather, they are aspects of ways of life, which all together bear on the question whether it is likely that abortion (for instance) will or will not become thought of as permissible. These aspects must be investigated for each case, rather than predicted *a priori*.

AN ALIEN TIDE?

Some of the current anxiety about abortion laws stems from the fear that habits or values from abroad are likely to sweep over Ireland. Fears of this sort are not entirely imaginary. Even if predictions are out of place, we do know something about what can be anticipated from the impact of large-scale contexts on smaller ones.

The 'modernisation thesis' – that as nations industrialise and democratise, they automatically converge culturally also – is no longer credible. But major alternative views do not offer much comfort either. We can see a core of economically powerful countries and concerns practising on the rest of the globe a 'cultural imperialism' even more insidious in its effects than old-style imperialism used to be. This imperialism bends legal systems before it and is not known for its humanitarian values; this raises serious issues about prospects for the existence and quality of human life in all parts of the world. Nonetheless its influence is not automatic, nor need it be yielded to inevitably.

Thus the present abortion debate in Ireland is far from the

neurotic affair it is sometimes presented as being. There is genuine concern about the effects of an anti-humanitarian cultural imperialism on Irish social contexts which are themselves undergoing rapid social and economic change. The political pluralism which, in the 1950s and 1960s, was supposed to constitute the invisible hand regulating moral, social and economic debate is no longer trusted automatically to supply social regulations which are worthy of respect. Yet it is not at all clear what social laws and institutions can effectively supply citizens with the optimum degree of control over their own lives while producing outcomes which do not undermine the moral virtues of this attempted 'good life'.

Those who wish to support human life and enhance its quality need much more practical knowledge about social contexts in which praxes affirming human life can be embedded. This knowledge, to be made effective, will have to be supplemented by an awareness of how people come to think, feel and believe the things they do: how it is that some moral positions come to be defended rather than others, and in what ways these interact with legal systems in the relevant contexts.

DIFFERENT GROUPS WITH DIFFERENT ARGUMENTS

Most of the current debates on the 'values' connected with legal structures fail to take into account, then, what values actually are. They are not special phenomena independent of other social formations, they do not exist in some separate value-world of their own where one value is affected only by another value. De Valera understood this when he advocated a particular economic way of life because he thought it would lead to a corresponding spiritual outlook. But the setting seen as hospitable to the dominant morality of De Valera's time is now apt to get short shrift from commentators – some of whom seem to feel uncomfortable with the idea of any connection at all between social context and argumentation.

But there is strong evidence of connections between forms of social life such as property systems, and morality. For instance, there are affinities between an astringent attitude to sexuality, or sensuality in general, and the practical pressures of post-Famine rural life, in particular the need for a system of inheritance which maintained farm sizes at a level which could sustain existence. Only one child of a farm family could be allowed to remain at home and have children; intimate decisions could not be made only on the basis of personal preference. For those for whom no work was available in service or in country towns, or for whom no dowry could be found (and at the end of the nineteenth century it was much less expensive to find the fare to America than to marry a Conamara farmer), there was a limited choice. Emigration might select out that portion of the population which baulked at the prospect of a celibate life in Ireland; or else there was the Church, or a chaste subsistence as a 'relative assisting' on the family farm. Over a quarter of the inhabitants of Ireland born about 1900 never married at all. This indicates, Irish historians say, a society with a high tolerance of sensual inactivity, and this lends a particular cast to the solutions to problems of reproductive morality which might seem most appropriate to the inhabitants of such a society.[1]

To point to the social setting within which a particular morality is situated is not to reduce morality to property relations. A particular practical position in the world may on the whole encourage people to see things in one way rather than another – moral values such as 'purity' can gain extra weight and apparent naturalness from having a role in a practical system of life. It is not entirely new to associate morality with matters of urgent concern for survival, such as economics – even though contemporary social and political discourse legitimises this connection with an overtness which may be novel.

If social settings can incline people to particular moral views, so can political ones. It is natural and necessary for nations attempting to escape from colonialism that they should pass through a phase of 'essentialism' in which their country is experienced, in opposition to its coloniser, as one, with a united set of beliefs and values. Such a phase may have reached its apogee in the years after Independence, and its gradual demise has coincided with a startlingly fast change in Irish social structure. Formerly, family property, particularly farm property, determined people's life

1. See David Fitzpatrick, 'Marriage in Post-Famine Ireland', and Brendan Walsh, 'Marriage in Ireland in the Twentieth Century', both in Art Cosgrave (ed.) *Marriage in Ireland*, 1988, Dublin, College Press; Richard Breen et al., *Understanding Contemporary Ireland*, 1990, Dublin, Gill and Macmillan; J. J. Lee, *Ireland 1912-1985: Politics and Society*, 1989, Cambridge, Cambridge University Press.

chances, whereas now the population is mainly dependent on employment in large organisations – radically different settings for discussion and debate.

This new class structure, which in other countries evolved over decades or centuries, has established itself here with a speed which has produced new social groups *unfamiliar* with each others' attitudes and values. The Republic no longer has the unified sense of values its inhabitants might have experienced between Independence and the 1950s (though the monolithic quality of thought even then has probably been exaggerated in memory).

Simultaneously, we are facing a sense of bankruptcy regarding many conventional methods for solving social dilemmas in a way which is both democratic and responsible. Different responses to these problems are likely to seem plausible to people at different social vantage points. To understand how this panorama of debate is developing we need more practical information on value-based aspects of behaviour and the ways in which debate about values is experienced in different parts of Irish society. If it is possible to understand the ways of life of which value-based attitudes form part, opposing views no longer look so abstract or so absurd, and communication of some sort can begin.

POLITICAL UNCERTAINTY

It may be that the much-publicised reluctance of politicians to take stands on issues of morality and law is attributable in part to their own social setting. Pressures are placed on them by a short-term election system, which means that the institutions of contemporary democracy themselves inhibit decision-making to the benefit of society. (This can be seen clearly in relation to environmental questions, which characteristically need long-term solutions.) Their reluctance is surely also related to a widespread uncertainty about what people in the country think and feel about matters of public moral concern.

Voting behaviour, for example, is not straightforward as an indicator of complex moral views. Irish electorates are by no means unusual in tending to vote for the status quo in referenda, but these should not be seen as mirrors of what people 'really' think. Referenda on social and moral questions often involve voter shifts from initial majorities in favour to eventual majorities against. This may not be because voters have changed their own moral views. Rather, reasonable doubts about a proposal can arise in cases of community conflict if political elites retreat from participating in debate. Thus, its sociopolitical context explains the result of the 1986 referendum on divorce, and we cannot read it as a straightforward account of the the views of the people.[2]

Other sources of information such as opinion polls show divisions among people's responses according to age, gender, and setting (urban or rural). But we do not know much about the ways of life in which these expressions are embedded or what people actually do themselves or tolerate in others.

As a preliminary to dialogue we need more knowledge of the views of these groups – and, as Professor Hannon points out, legal methods alone are not necessarily the best method of fostering such communication.[3] This implies that politicians may hesitate in part because they are not the most appropriate people to act; legal prohibitions may not be our last bastion against an unbridled contempt for human existence.

VALUES, THE LAW, AND THE POSITION OF WOMEN

It is unproductive to discuss abortion without regard to the social settings in which people view it as they do; in particular, we need to know more about the settings in which people are likely to choose it. A tendency to opt for abortion should not be disconnected from other aspects of women's situation; for example, the fact that it is hard for women to achieve social respect or to fulfil their own capacities at the same time as having children. Both the daily structure of work in industrial society and the peak expected years of achievement make the demands of childrearing and those of high-status work incompatible.

The Constitution appears to accord an special status to childrearing when it lays down that mothers should not be forced by economic necessity to go and look for work. This is in principle a law, but has never been taken seriously. In fact Mary Daly shows[4] that provisions to deal with dire economic necessity among women imply that mothers are either respectably maintained by

2. R. Darcy and Michael Laver, 'Referendum Dynamics and the Irish Divorce Amendment', *Public Opinion Quarterly*, vol. 54, 1990, 1-20.
3. Patrick Hannon, *Church, State, Morality and Law*, 1992, Dublin, Gill and Macmillan, p. 115.
4. Mary Daly, *Women and Poverty*, 1989, Dublin, Attic Press and Combat Poverty Agency.

their husbands, or else victims or whores.

Nor does it appear that the wisdom and authority which women can offer are likely to be enthusiastically incorporated into legal institutions. Aspects of the public world with high profile, and high impact on women, such as medicine, are arranged by men and seen from the point of view of men. Adult participation in the contemporary world, in a word, is not highly associated with qualities and experiences perceived as characteristically feminine; and this must yield a setting for debate which weakens women's willingness to tolerate extreme suffering for the sake of these qualities and experiences.

This disavowal of female authority in public life is not compensated for by effective 'complementary' recognition of the special spheres to which women are relegated. It is frequently remarked that, despite the apparent desire of the Constitution to protect the position of women and families in Ireland, laws actually enforcing such protection have been slow to arrive and have often been established under pressure from Irish lawyers or the EC rather than from the Dáil.

None of this implies that current argumentation, steered from a masculine vantage point, necessarily works for the good of men. The contemporary orientation of work towards male lives pressurises men emotionally to desert their families and to support moral and legal conventions in which the preciousness of their children is not recognised. In practice, it is hard to see how the position in society of women and children can be argued for effectively while men are prevented from taking more part in child-rearing – but this could not be done without a radical restructuring of the world of work.

Legal measures would certainly assist here. Indeed it is difficult to see that the situation could be changed without them – even if it is unlikely that they could alter established social attitudes by themselves. Without social and legal settings encouraging men to value children and the work of caring for them, it seems much less likely that this work or the children it deals with will acquire effective social protection.

HOW TO BRING ABOUT DIALOGUE

It is crucial in this situation of argument and counter-argument to recall that debates about laws and morals are themselves social occurrences. There are at least three broadly accepted views of what arguing is – three positions between which people slide so rapidly as not to notice it themselves.

First, there is the view that argument is the exchange of what can universally be established as good reasons, where it does not matter who the arguer is or what position in society he or she occupies – the strength of respective arguments alone is to determine the outcome, and the integrity of the arguer lies in making an argument clear to others.

The drawbacks of this view are twofold. First, it encourages speakers to see anyone who does not in the end agree with them as mad or bad. A universalist understanding of moral argument thus risks failing to understand most of the social dimensions of real-life argumentation. But, secondly, many criteria which are claimed to be universal can on investigation be revealed as the social, political or moral views of some dominant group. Persons who make this discovery are often so disillusioned by their unmasking of cultural imperialisms that they fall into total relativism instead. This view of argument does not cope well, then, with the discovery that criteria for what is relevant, what is convincing, what is obvious, and so forth, are strongly affected by social locations and affinities.

In my opinion this understanding of arguing can be rescued, by admitting that we know much less about the criteria for good arguments than we may have assumed, but that this does not imply that no such criteria exist. This position involves making clear the provisional nature of some of our arguments and the element of commitment, rather than certainty, in our support for others. The question of commitment, moreover, involves trying to convince others of the human productiveness of a practice, rather than bludgeoning them into recognising the certainty of a fact.

The second view of argument relevant here is a more completely sociological one, investigating arguments in terms of their relations to their settings, without committing the investigator to their rightness or wrongness. This involves a systematic suspension of disbelief such as many people experience, for example, in relation to foreign cultures: we feel we can see why they see things as they do, even if we would not propose to adopt such a course for ourselves.

Such a stance is necessary as a preliminary to successful moral dialogue, for otherwise it is impossible to understand the position of those one is communicating with or why they are taking it up.

It is nonetheless a difficult attitude to sustain without retreat into relativism – abandoning belief in the possibility of reasonable support for any given argument rather than another. If this aimless approach to debate is avoided, there is the even commoner danger of unconsciously dividing humanity into two sorts: those who maintain different views, but this does not matter because they belong to another group – foreigners or those who are not co-religionists – and one's own people. The latter, of course, are expected to agree with one's own taken-for-granted conception of how the world is. To relinquish the automatic bestowal of sacrality on one's own worldview without abandoning all moral commitments is difficult. Hence the understandable trepidation of those who fear that to abandon the claims to certainty of their own moral positions is to fall prey to a bankrupt pluralism. But without suspending attachment to the naturalness of one's own views, it is hardly possible to enter into dialogue with those of a different tradition.

Finally, traditional societies view arguments as indissolubly linked to social position: priests exist to provide one category of argument, school teachers another, and so on, and there is no question of just anyone devising an argument which is better than the local teacher's and thereby claiming to have a say in school business. In this view, integrity and responsibility consist in the moral and emotional commitment of the occupants of these social roles to the good of those they serve – and by no means in attempting to explain to others the reasons for their decisions, which are regarded as nobody's business but theirs.

The disadvantages of this view are many, but in particular its refusal to acknowledge the relevance of an argument if the wrong person puts it forward. On the other hand, this position does recognise something ignored by the universalist view – namely, how important in arguing is a justified trust in the personal commitments of the other person. This is rarely expressed in the contemporary world, for the traditional view is disappearing in Western society, but – especially in relation to religious arguments – it has not entirely expired.

It adds considerably to the confusion of public debate that protagonists switch rapidly and unnoticed from one of these three views to the next – people should not pronounce on such-and-such a subject because they are not priests, or not women; we can understand how the British or the Dutch might behave but that has no relevance to ourselves; it is possible to see that other people's views might have evolved within some special social setting, but not our own.

UNDERSTANDING THE OTHER

Amalgamating the virtues of all three views, it is possible to admit that different social contexts do encourage their own particular ways of seeing and evaluating what is going on, of establishing patterns of relevance and emphasis – and without losing sight of one's own position, to investigate the human interactions such patterns encourage. These patterns reinforce directly taught morality because they in part constitute value-positions. The distinction between facts and values is anything but absolute: to attend for ninety per cent of one's time to the rights of unborn children, and not at all to those of children once they are born, is to indicate that the former are more important – and *vice versa*.

To understand other people's points of view, without which it is hardly possible to communicate with, let alone convince them, it is therefore necessary to attend to the practical details of social contexts in which their views arise. To increase effective support for children at all stages of their development, it is necessary to study the sorts of context in which people wish to give this support. Only at this point shall we be in a position to imagine the details of a legal framework which genuinely supports these developments at the same time as encouraging full, active participation in public life.

The Conscience of the Voter and Law-maker

PATRICK HANNON

The complexity of the situation produced by the Supreme Court decision in the case of *The Attorney General -v- X and Others* almost defies summary. The main ingredients now are the Maastricht Treaty, the scope of the Protocol and – underlying and permeating all detail – the constitutional law on abortion. As I write, the Government is considering how best to make sense of it even provisionally; and it would be foolish indeed to predict the course on which its decisions will set us.

It follows that an essay upon ethical aspects of our society's predicament must remain at a somewhat abstract level. But perhaps there is merit in this. For it counters the danger of hasty assessment from outside, and it underscores the point that the bearers of responsibility for an appropriate ethical resolution are the citizens and rulers of our land. The challenge to each of us is inescapable; the answers will not fall from the sky.

But even an abstract reflection may help a little. The general lines of the problematic are not unfamiliar, for all that its detail seems overwhelming just now. The heart of the task is the embodiment of moral value in the law, a problem which every society must cope with. In a pluralist culture the question is inevitable: whose morality, what law? We have had a recurring experience of that question during the past two decades; though perhaps it is worth making the point at the outset that it is a mistake to think that Ireland is peculiar in this regard.

COMPLICATIONS

It does of course take on a local colour here, the colour of an issue in Church-State relations. And the reason for this is not hard to find. Morality is commonly taken to be the province of 'Church', law the business of 'State'; and these institutions are commonly identified with their leaderships. An additional complication arises in a country in which one Church is that of the majority. In Ireland a Church-State matter is almost invariably perceived as (and almost invariably is) a matter of the relationships between institutions of State and those of the Roman Catholic Church.

It cannot therefore be surprising that a reflection on the conscience of the voter in an Irish context must have a special eye to the Catholic voter. But again at the outset it is as well to signal that a pivotal point of the argument of this piece is that the central question for the Catholic voter is in principle no different than for anyone else. For the central challenge is that of harmonising individual freedoms with the claims of a common good. And that, as already intimated, is a task in every society and the business of every citizen, irrespective of moral or religious persuasion.

I hope to explain and establish this contention in due course but it is probably necessary to acknowledge now that the Catholic's position is, on the face of it, complicated by two factors. The first is that there are some moral beliefs which though they may be shared by others are not unfairly regarded as characteristically Catholic: the belief that human life is sacred from the moment of conception is an obvious instance. The second is that Catholics are used to a hierarchical leadership in morals as well as in matters of faith.

CATHOLIC LAW FOR A CATHOLIC PEOPLE?

The first of these factors gives rise to the question whether it is inevitable, where there is a Catholic majority, that Catholic moral beliefs are enshrined in the the law of the land. This may be answered shortly in the words of the Bishops' Conference in a statement of 1976:

> It is not the view of the Catholic hierarchy that, in the law of the State, the principles peculiar to *our* faith should be made binding on people who do not adhere to that faith.

But the Conference went on to offer a view on a proposal to change the law (on divorce, as it happened), making it clear that the bishops did not favour the proposal.

And so arises a second question: when the Conference makes its position on a legislative measure known, is *that* view binding on the Catholic conscience? A short answer must again suffice here, this time taken from a 1983 statement on what was to become the Eighth Amendment:

> We recognise the right of each person to vote according to conscience. Each voter has the responsibility of weighing the moral

consequences of his or her vote and of making a conscientious decision in the privacy of the polling booth.

It will doubtless be recalled that the Conference also set out its own view of the proposed measure in emphatic terms.

What in these cases is the Catholic to think or do? On the one hand the bishops say that the vote, in the Oireachtas or in the polling booth, is a matter for the conscientious judgment of citizen or politician. On the other hand they, official custodians of the Catholic tradition, take a clear position on the acceptability or otherwise of a measure as they see it. Some critics tax them with failure of nerve: there should be no suggestion that a Catholic is free to go against the bishops' view. Others dismiss the Conference's approach as a new and only slightly more sophisticated way of telling the voter what to do.

RELIGIOUS AND MORAL FREEDOM

It may be that some of the difficulties which some people have with the bishops' approach have their origin in the lack of a framework in which to consider the question, how is a Catholic to vote when it comes to the enshrining of moral beliefs in the law?

People are no doubt generally aware that there is a difference between morality and law, and that not everything immoral ought to be illegal. But there is an uncertainty as to what principles should guide us in deciding *which* immorality should be proscribed. We are not at ease with the question, whose morality, what law?

I should like to suggest here that there is in contemporary Catholic theology that makings of a methodology which can help the voter cope with this question. It will not yield neat answers; yet it should, I think, help set the questioner on the right lines. It is to be found in the official teachings of the Church, in the *Declaration on Religious Freedom* of the Second Vatican Council. The Council affirmed a right to religious freedom, and I shall argue that what it says applies, *mutatis mutandis,* in the moral sphere too.

AFFIRMING THE LAY CONSCIENCE

But first some brief theological considerations regarding two pertinent themes, the role of laity and the teaching function of the bishops. The Vatican Council elsewhere spoke of an 'autonomy of earthly affairs', in reference to the laws and methods proper to the various areas of human knowing and acting.[1] And later it observed that 'It is to the laity, though not exclusively to them, that secular duties and activity properly belong'. [2] Accordingly it is the business of the layperson 'to cultivate a properly informed conscience and to impress the divine law on the affairs of the earthly city'.

Plainly the Council wished to affirm secular value and lay competence, and it wished also to place the role of the cleric as such in proper perspective.

For guidance and spiritual direction let them turn to the clergy: but let them realise that their pastors will not always be so expert as to have a ready answer to every problem ...: this is not the role of the clergy: it is rather up to [laypeople] to shoulder their responsibilities under the guidance of Christian wisdom and with eager attention to the teaching authority of the Church.

But the teaching authority is itself required to acknowledge the 'autonomy of earthly affairs'. It remains the task of the hierarchy to preach the Gospel and to teach the faith and its ways. Yet it cannot supply for the lay vocation; and when its teachings moves from the core of the faith into the detail of practical living it will not have 'a ready answer to every problem'. It is indeed at that stage especially beholden to secular experience and distinctively lay expertise.

What is here at stake was well expressed in the US Bishops' pastoral on war and peace.

As Catholic bishops we write this letter as an exercise of our teaching ministry.... We wish to explore and explain the resources of the moral religious teaching and to apply it to specific questions of our day. *In doing this we realise, and we want readers of this letter to recognise, that not all statements in this letter have the same moral authority* [italics mine].[3]

1. *Gaudium et Spes* par. 36.Tr. at p. 935 in A. Flannery, O.P. (ed), *Vatican Council II. The Conciliar and Post-Conciliar Documents.* Vatican Collection, Vol. 1, New Revised Edition. Dublin: Dominican Publications. 1992 (hereinafter Flannery).
2. This and the next two quotations are from *Gaudium et Spes*, 43, Flannery, p. 944.
3. *The Challenge of Peace* (Washington 1983). Cf p. 249 in Murnion, Philip J. (ed.) *Catholics and Nuclear War* (London 1983).

The point is amplified in the sentences which follow:

> At times we state universally binding moral principles found in the teaching of the Church: at other times the pastoral letter makes specific applications, observations which allow for diversity of opinion on the part of those who assess the factual data of a situation differently. However, we expect Catholics to give our moral judgments serious consideration when they are forming their own views on specific problems.

Such in brief is part of the immediate theological background to the focal question of this article: how is a Catholic expected to vote upon matters involving what is usually called the enforcement of morality by the law? I said earlier that a starting-point is furnished by the *Declaration on Religious Freedom* of Vatican II, and now we must see how this is so.[4]

PERSONAL DIGNITY AND THE SEARCH FOR TRUTH

The core of the Council's teaching in the *Declaration* is that in religious matters people shouldn't be forced to go against conscience nor should they be stopped from acting according to conscience 'within due limits'.[5] The limits turn out to be the requirements of the common good, the touchstones of which according to a standard Catholic account are peace, justice and public morality. It is obvious that our attention must focus closely on the significance of these limitations, but first it is necessary to indicate the basis for the Council's teaching and to show that what it says about religious freedom may be transposed to the domain of morals.

The Council bases its teaching on the dignity of the person and on the nature of the search for truth. There are supplementary considerations arising from the nature of religious faith and from the way in which Jesus preached the gospel message to the first hearers.

But it is the 'philosophical' basis which is ultimate, and it is on this basis that it can be argued that the Council's principles extend to morality too. For the dignity of the human person must be always be upheld, and whether in religion or in morals the character of the human search for truth is essentially the same.

---

4. What follows is treated extensively in my *Church, State, Morality and Law*, (Dublin: Gill and Macmillan, 1992).
5. *Dignitatis Humanae* in Flannery 799-812. cf esp. 800.

On the analogy of the Council's teaching on religious freedom therefore one might formulate a principle somewhat as follows:

> In matters of moral belief and practice people shouldn't be made to go against their consciences, nor should they be prevented from acting according to conscience, subject to the requirements of the common good.

It is obvious that the import of the proviso is crucial.

THE COMMON GOOD

The common good is a complex concept whose roots lie deep in Christian theology, but in modern Catholic social teaching it is often used to designate the ensemble of conditions of life in society which facilitate the person's flourishing. As already mentioned, some purchase may be got upon its concrete meaning by reference to the requirements of peace, justice and public morality. The component which has most relevance in our context is public morality.

What is being asserted then is that when a Catholic is faced with the question what morality should be reflected in or enforced by the law of the land, he or she has a starting-point, by analogy, in the Council's basic principle about religious freedom. The starting-point may be formulated by saying that the law shouldn't force people to act against their consciences, nor restrain them from acting according to conscience, unless what they have in mind is at odds with 'public morality'.

But this principle – and all the questions to which its concrete application gives rise – is not peculiar to Catholics. John Stuart Mill and James Fitzjames Stephen debated a version of it in the nineteenth century, and H.L.A. Hart and Lord Devlin are only two from among those who have discussed it in our time.[6] That is why I said at the outset that, for all that in Ireland as elsewhere it takes on a local colour, the task for the Catholic is the same as for every citizen.

WHAT IS PUBLIC MORALITY?

We are of course left with the question, what is public morality? It may be important to say that it is not necessarily the morality of

---

6. Patrick Devlin, *The Enforcement of Morals* (Oxford 1965). H.L.A. Hart, *Law, Liberty and Morality* (Oxford 1963).

the majority, for the impression is sometimes given that the fact that a moral belief is held by a majority is sufficient to warrant its imposition by law.

Lord Devlin came near that view when he said that every society is held together by its subscription to a corpus of moral value and principle, recognisable by reference to the standard of the reasonable man (sic), and which it is the business of the law to enforce. Yet he did not quite adopt it, for he thought also that in deciding what morality is to be imposed the lawmaker should display some preference for freedom and for privacy.

Professor Hart, for whom individual freedom is paramount, offered a version of the harm principle: unless behaviour is demonstrably injurious it should not be proscribed.

Which to choose? This is not the place to try to persuade to a choice, but rather to make only one point. Devlin's is the conservative, Hart's a standard liberal view; but neither view is especially the Catholic. A Catholic can take either, and he/she will have the same problems with each as will anyone else. Again it seems worth making what to some will seem a trite point: the Christian is not tied to philosophical or political orthodoxies.

In this connection it is *à propos* to recall words of another document of Vatican II, its *Constitution on the Church in the Modern World*:

> Very often [the layperson's] Christian vision will suggest a certain solution in some given situation. Yet it happens rather frequently, and legitimately so, that some of the faithful, with no less sincerity, will see the problem quite differently. Now if one or other of the proposed solutions is too easily associated with the message of the Gospel, they ought to remember that in those cases no one is permitted to identify the authority of the Church exclusively with his own opinion. Let them, then, try to guide each other by sincere dialogue in a spirit of mutual charity and with anxious interest above all in the common good.[7]

GUIDELINES

But are there any guidelines for a conscientious attempt to decide what law in a given matter we should have? It is not, I think, a small gain to be able to avail ourselves of the framework and principles afforded by the *Declaration on Religious Freedom;* the fact that

---

7. *Gaudium et Spes* 43, Flannery 944.

we are thereby committed to a respect for the values and views of those from whom we differ is not its least important benefit.

And even if the approaches of Devlin or Hart will not produce instant solutions we may recognise our own stances, in their limitations as well as in their strengths, in the arguements made by each. But are there any more specific guidelines?

There are, for example, what Lord Devlin described in *The Enforcement of Morals* as 'elastic principles' – a bias toward freedom and privacy, a reluctance to run with fashion, a modest expectation of what law can do.

Those who favour the more liberal approach of Hart may be helped by questions suggested by Simon Lee:

1. What is the harm (from which there is question of giving legal protection)?
2. Who or what is harmed?
3. How serious is the harm?
4. Are there countervailing benefits?
5. Do those harmed need or deserve society's protection?
6. What level of protection is most appropriate, bearing in mind the costs or disadvantages?[8]

COMMUNITY CONSENT

John Courtney Murray, architect of the Council's *Declaration*, offered another kind of criterion:

A legal ban on evil must consider what St Thomas calls its own 'possibility'. That is, will the ban be obeyed, at least by the generality? Is it enforceable against the disobedient? Is it prudent to undertake the enforcement of this or that ban, in view of the possibility of harmful effects in other areas of social life? Is the instrumentality of coercive law a good means for the eradication of this or that social vice? And, since a means is not a good means if it fails to work in most cases, what are the lessons of experience in the matter? What is the prudent view of results – the long view or the short view?[9]

An underlying theme in Murray's treatment is that of community consent: in the absence of backing by the people 'law either with-

---

8. Simon Lee, *Law and Morals* (Oxford 1986), p. 34.
9. John C. Murray, S.J., *We Hold These Truths* (New York 1960), pp. 166-167.

ers away or becomes tyrannical'. This is true of every community but in a religiously pluralist society it achieves crucial significance:

> Basic religious divisions lead to conflict of moral views; certain asserted 'rights' clash with other 'rights' no less strongly asserted. And the divergences are often irreducible (p. 168).

Murray believed that the public consensus should include agreement on rules to regulate the interrelationships of the divergent groups, as well as their common relation to the order of law.

He proposed four such rules, and though he was speaking about the specific question of censorship of the arts and literature, Richard McBrien has suggested that the rules have a more general application.[10]

First, each group has the right to demand conformity from its own members.

Second, no group in a pluralist society has the right to expect that government will impose or prohibit some act of behaviour in the absence of support in society at large.

Third, any group has the right to work toward a change in moral standards, through the use of methods of persuasion and pacific argument.

Fourth, no group has a right to impose its religious or moral views on others by force, coercion or violence.

MEANS AND ENDS

I began this piece by adverting to what just now seems an intractable complexity in the facts of the situation which has followed the Supreme Court's judgment in *The Attorney General -v- X. and Others*. Some of that complexity will, it may be hoped, unravel as individual elements in the situation are in their turn opened to scrutiny and to action. But the moral challenge remains daunting, for we shall have to try not only to achieve a morally defensible resolution but to do so in a morally creditable way.

I hope that the foregoing may help in the task of putting down some markers. But a prayer for wisdom, courage and forbearance seems in order.

---

10. Richard P. McBrien, *Caesar's Coin* (New York 1987), pp. 165,166.

Abortion and the Law

GERRY WHYTE

There is surely one point, at least, on which participants in this most divisive of debates can agree, namely that the moral and legal issues involved are incredibly complex. The complexity of the legal issues, which is the focus of this paper, stems, in part, from the fact that we are dealing with legal texts in respect of which we do not yet have any authoritative interpretation. Nor is clarity of thought aided by the rapid and bewildering rate of developments in recent weeks. Disappointing though it may be for those readers who are seeking definitive answers to the various legal issues raised in the current debate, I have had to set for myself a much more modest (though attainable) objective: I hope to set out, in an ordered form, the main legal issues thrown up by the present situation, together with a summary of the conflicting points of view. In this task, I have benefitted greatly from the various comments published by legal academics and practitioners during recent weeks in the national newspapers.[1]

It will be useful if, at this juncture, I attend to three preliminary matters. First, I will set out the relevant legal texts on the area. These are art.40.3.3 of the Irish Constitution, Protocol No.17 to the Maastricht Treaty [hereafter 'the Protocol'] and, finally, the Solemn Declaration signed on 1 May 1992 by the Foreign Ministers of the EC member States.[2]

Art.40.3.3 provides:

> The State acknowledges the right to life of the unborn and, with due regard to the equal right to life of the mother, guarantees in its laws to respect, and, as far as practicable, by its laws to defend and vindicate that right.

1. I am particularly indebted to James Kingston and Anthony Whelan for providing me with a copy of their comprehensive and informative article, "The Protection of the Unborn in Three Legal Orders", prior to its publication in the April 1992 issue of the *Irish Law Times*.

2. Statutory regulation of abortion is limited at present to s.58 of the Offences Against the Person Act 1861. This provision was considered by Mr. Justice McNaughten in the U.K. in *R. v. Bourne* [1939] 1 K.B. 687 wherein he directed a jury that a termination of pregnancy performed in the belief that it was necessary to prevent the mother from becoming a physical or mental wreck was not an offence under the section. The relevance, if any, of this case in Irish law is considered below at footnote 10.

The Protocol states:

> Nothing in the Treaty on the European Union or in the Treaties establishing the European Communities or in the Treaties or Acts modifying or supplementing those Treaties shall affect the application in Ireland of Article 40.3.3 of the Constitution of Ireland.

Finally, the Solemn Declaration reads:

> The High Contracting Parties to the Treaty on European Union signed at Maastricht on the 7th day of February 1992
> Having considered the terms of Protocol No.17 to the said Treaty on European Union which is annexed to that Treaty and to the Treaties establishing the European Communities
> Hereby give the following legal interpretation:
> that it was and is their intention that the Protocol shall not limit freedom either to travel between member States or, in accordance with conditions which may be laid down in conformity with Community law, by Irish legislation, to obtain or make available in Ireland information relating to services lawfully available in member States.
> At the same time the High Contracting Parties solemnly declare that, in the event of a future constitutional amendment in Ireland which concerns the subject matter of Article 40.3.3 of the Constitution of Ireland and which does not conflict with the intention of the High Contracting Parties hereinbefore expressed, they will, following the entry into force of the Treaty on European Union, be favourably disposed to amending the said Protocol so as to extend its application to such constitutional amendment if Ireland so requests.

DIRECT AND INDIRECT INTENTION

The second preliminary matter is to define abortion for the purposes of this paper. I use the term to signify the medical treatment of a pregnant woman which results in the death, either directly or indirectly, of the foetus. It should be apparent from this that it ignores the traditional distinction drawn in Catholic moral theology between medical interventions procuring the death of the foetus directly and those which have as a secondary and undesired consequence the termination of the pregnancy. Such a distinction is not known to Irish law.

BACKGROUND

Finally, it might assist the reader's comprehension of this area if I set out, very briefly, the sequence of legal developments leading up to the current situation. Prior to 1983, abortion in Ireland was prohibited by s.58 of the Offences against the Person Act 1861 which made it a criminal offence to procure a miscarriage. In 1983, this criminal prohibition of abortion was joined by the constitutional guarantee, in art.40.3.3, of the right to life of the unborn. That constitutional provision was considered by the courts for the first time in The *Attorney General (SPUC (Ireland) Ltd) v. Open Door Counselling Ltd*[3] in the context of the dissemination of information on abortion services. The Supreme Court granted an injunction restraining the defendants from assisting pregnant women 'to travel abroad to obtain abortions by referral to a clinic, by the making of their travel arrangements or by informing them of the identity and location and method of communication with a specified clinic or clinics'. The defendants subsequently brought a case under the European Convention on Human Rights.[4] In the initial stage of this procedure, the European Commission on Human Rights held, by a majority of eight to five, that Irish law did violate art.10 of the Convention, guaranteeing freedom of expression, because the activities of the defendants were not proscribed by law, the terms of art.40.3.3 being insufficiently precise for this purpose. Three of the majority Commissioners also took the view that the Irish measures went beyond what was necessary in a democratic society because they were disproportionate. In this context, it was noted that a ban on information was ineffective in protecting the right to life of the unborn in the absence of a ban on travel.

In order to preserve, albeit somewhat loosely, the chronological sequence of events, I turn now to consider the subsequent

---

3. [1988] I.R. 593

4. Not to be confused with the European Community. The European Convention on Human Rights was signed first in 1950 and has been ratified by 19 of the 21 member States of the Council of Europe. Proceedings taken under the Convention are dealt with initially by the European Commission on Human Rights which decides on admissibility of the claim and then, if a friendly settlement between the parties is not forthcoming, issues an opinion as to whether there has been a violation of the Convention. The matter may then be referred within a period of three months to the European Court of Human Rights for an authoritative decision as to whether such a violation has taken place.

treatment of art.40.3.3 by the Irish courts before describing briefly the next stage in the *Open Door Counselling* case before the Court of Human Rights.

Article 40.3.3 came before the Supreme Court on two further occasions in 1989 and again the context was the dissemination of information on abortion services. In *SPUC (Ireland) Ltd v. Coogan*,[5] the Supreme Court held that the plaintiff society had sufficient legal standing to bring an action enforcing compliance with art.40.3.3. In *SPUC (Ireland) Ltd v. Grogan*[6] the society had sought an injunction restraining members of three students' unions from distributing certain information in relation to abortion services available outside the State. Miss Justice Carroll, in the High Court, exercised her discretion to refer the case to the Court of Justice of the European Community, for advice on certain aspects of EC law before coming to a final conclusion. In the interim, she made no express order refusing or adjourning the application for the injunction. The plaintiff appealed to the Supreme Court against this failure of the High Court to grant an injunction pending receipt of the opinion from the Court of Justice which, it was agreed, would take a minimum of eighteen months. The Supreme Court ruled, *inter alia*, that the fact that the case had been referred to the Court of Justice did not automatically have the effect of postponing a decision on whether or not to grant an injunction on a holding basis and they granted such an injunction to last until the final determination of the action.

On 4 October 1991, the Court of Justice ruled, in answer to the questions posed by Miss Justice Carroll, that termination of pregnancy, performed in accordance with the law of the State in which it is carried out, constituted a service within the meaning of art.60 of the Treaty. The Court went on to hold that it was not contrary to EC law for Ireland to prohibit the defendants from distributing information about abortion clinics in other jurisdictions where those clinics have no involvement in the distribution of the said information. The clear implication of this ruling is that agencies having a commercial relationship with abortion clinics are entitled, under EC law, to disseminate information about the services provided.

Apparently as a result of this decision, the Government was per-

5. [1989] I.R. 734.
6. [1989] I.R. 753.

suaded to lobby for the adoption of what eventually became Protocol No.17 to the Maastricht Treaty. This Treaty was signed on 7 February 1992.

Ten days later, Mr Justice Costello granted an injunction restraining a 14 year old girl, pregnant as a result of an alleged rape, from travelling to the U.K. in order to have an abortion – *Attorney General v. X*. The subsequent unprecedented public reaction was in the main hostile and the case brought the abortion question firmly back onto the Irish agenda. However, because of the existence of the Protocol, it quickly became apparent that there was more at stake than just a national policy on abortion. A right to travel to obtain services, grounded on EC law, was seen as a possible 'escape route' for the girl and her family. The Protocol, however, purported to take EC law out of the equation and, on one view, this meant that someone like X would not be able to invoke a right to travel under EC law if the Protocol was ever ratified. Thus ratification of Maastricht by the Irish electorate was threatened by the implications of Mr Justice Costello's decision.

The case was appealed to the Supreme Court where, on 26 February, a majority of the Court held that the injunction should be lifted, the judgments being delivered on 5 March.[7] The majority judgments held that the right to life of the unborn had to be balanced against the right to life of the mother and that, in the present case, where the mother was threatening to commit suicide, the law should not prevent her having an abortion. All of the judges eschewed any reliance on EC law, on the basis that the case was capable of being resolved solely under domestic law.[8] However three members of the Court did indicate, in comments which do not form part of the binding *ratio* of the decision, that the constitutional right to travel under domestic law could be restrained in order to prevent an abortion taking place abroad.

The judgments appear to have pleased no one. Those who had campaigned for the introduction of art.40.3.3 in 1983 were dis-

7. Supreme Court, 5 March 1992. The judgments of the High and Supreme Court, together with the submissions made to the Supreme Court, are contained in *Attorney General v. X and Others*, ed. S. McDonagh, Incorporated Council of Law Reporting for Ireland, 1992.

8. One practical implication of this approach was that the Supreme Court was then under no obligation to seek the advice of the European Court of Justice as to the impact of EC law on the case, a process which would have delayed final resolution of the issues raised in *X* by as much as eighteen months.

mayed at the latitude given to the mother's right to life while their opponents were concerned about the possibility that, if the Protocol was ratified, pregnant women seeking abortions abroad, whose lives were not endangered by the pregnancy, could be restrained from travelling by the State. The decision in X also had implications for the existing constitutional ban on the dissemination of information about abortion services abroad as it seemed to follow from the Supreme Court ruling that women whose lives were at risk could not lawfully be denied such information. Indeed, on 24 March 1992, counsel for the State expressly conceded that such was the case in argument before the European Court of Human Rights in the *Open Door Counselling Ltd* case.

After some initial hesitation, the Government decided to seek an amendment to the Protocol which would ensure that EC law rights to travel and information would continue to be available to Irish citizens after ratification of the Maastricht Treaty. The other member States refused to re-open debate on the Protocol for fear that this might set a precedent for the re-negotiation of other aspects of the Maastricht Treaty. Consequently, the Government had to settle for a Solemn Declaration of the intentions of the High Contracting Parties on the matter of the Protocol.[9]

The most recent development in this saga was the statement, on 23 April 1992, by the Taoiseach, Mr Albert Reynolds, T.D., that if the Maastricht Treaty (including the Protocol) was approved in the forthcoming referendum on 18 June, the Attorney General would seek no further injunctions to stop women from travelling abroad. This, apparently, was based on the Attorney General's 'practical interpretation' of the Solemn Declaration that the Irish people would, in approving the Maastricht Treaty, have voted in favour of a right to travel.

At the time of writing, we await, first, the outcome of the referendum on Maastricht to be held on 18 June; second, the publication of the terms of a constitutional amendment on the right to travel and to information, in respect of which a referendum is promised for later in the year; third, the publication of legislation and/or the terms of a constitutional referendum on the substantive issue of a right to abortion, and, finally, the delivery of the decision of the Court of Human Rights in the *Open Door Counselling*

---

9. This Solemn Declaration was formally adopted by the EC foreign ministers on 1 May 1992.

Ltd case, which is expected to be handed down in the next six months or so.

Having outlined the sequence of events leading to the present situation, I now turn to describe the complex legal problems thrown up by these developments. I propose to consider each of the following in turn – first, in what circumstances may one lawfully obtain an abortion in this jurisdiction? ; second, what restrictions, if any, exist on the right to travel abroad in order to obtain an abortion?; and, finally, is there a right to receive and disseminate, within this jurisdiction, information on abortion facilities? For each question, I will consider the impact of national law, the European Convention on Human Rights and EC law.

LAWFUL ABORTIONS IN IRELAND

National Law

The litmus test for determining when abortions may lawfully be carried out in Ireland is contained in the majority judgments in *Attorney General v. X*[10] which essentially hold that abortion is permissible where continuance of the pregnancy constitutes a real and substantial risk to the life of the mother.[11] This legal proposi-

---

10. One of the more obscure aspects of this whole debate is to what extent, if at all, the U.K. decision in *R. v. Bourne* [1939] 1 K.B. 687 represents the law in Ireland. In that case, McNaughten J. directed the jury that, in relation to a criminal prosecution taken under s.58 of the Offences Against the Person Act 1861, the prosecution had to prove beyond reasonable doubt that the abortion had not been carried out in good faith in order to preserve the life of the mother. A passage in this summing up is capable of being construed as interpreting the right to life of the mother as encompassing a quality of life, over and beyond a mere physical existence, As to the possible relevance of this case to Irish law, it should be pointed out, first, that as a foreign authority it can, at most, have only persuasive value for an Irish judge and, second, that a direction to a jury does not constitute part of the *ratio decidendi* , i.e., the binding element, of a decision. In the Supreme Court, Mr Justice O'Flaherty stated that the enactment of Art.40.3.3 did not bring about any fundamental change in the law but, at the same time, he did not indicate whether *Bourne* correctly represented the pre-1983 position in Ireland. On the other hand, Mr Justice McCarthy appeared to consider that s.58 constituted an absolute ban on abortion while the Chief Justice, Mr Justice Finlay, emphasised in his test for lawful abortions that there had to be a real and substantial risk to the life, as distinct from the health, of the mother. By implication, this would appear to reject the broader interpretation of *Bourne*. In any event, given that *X* was decided on the basis of a threat to life rather than to quality of life, its *ratio decidendi* cannot extend to permitting abortions where there is only a threat to the quality of life of the mother, as opposed to a threat to her actual physical existence.
11. While the formulation of the test varies slightly from judge to judge, noth-

tion, of itself, could hardly be regarded as surprising, given the reference in art.40.3.3 to the need to balance the right to life of the unborn with that of the mother. What may, perhaps, be regarded as surprising about the majority verdict was the treatment of a threat of suicide as a real and substantial risk to the life of the mother.[12]

How far does X go in permitting lawful abortions in Ireland? First of all, an abortion may only be lawfully carried out where the person performing the operation has a *bona fide* belief that the mother's life is threatened by the continuation of the pregnancy. It has been suggested by some commentators that this essentially precludes any criminal prosecution for having performed an abortion, on the ground that it will be impossible for the State to prove that the defendant did not have such a *bona fide* belief. Undoubtedly it is difficult for a prosecutor to prove beyond any reasonable doubt what the subjective intention of the defendant was at the time the operation was performed. However it is for the jury to decide guilt or innocence and if there is sufficient evidence available, which proves the matter beyond all reasonable doubt, the jury may choose to disbelieve the defendant's claim, that he held a *bona fide* belief that the operation was necessary to save the life of the mother.

Another fear expressed about X is that it permits an abortion at any stage of the pregnancy. This is based on the fact that the majority judgments do not specify any time limits after which abortions may not lawfully be carried out.

The fallacy in this argument is to assume that silence on the matter of time limits implies that no time limits exist at all. A case is only a binding legal authority for the legal proposition necessary to decide the issues raised by the material facts before the

---

ing of significance turns on these variations. The dissenting judge, Mr Justice Hederman, ruled that before an abortion could lawfully take place, 'the evidence required to justify the [abortion] must be of such a weight and cogency as to leave open no other conclusion but that the consequences of the continuance of the pregnancy will, to an extremely high degree of probability, cost the mother her life and that any such opinion must be based on the most competent medical opinion available.' In his opinion, the evidence actually before the Court did not satisfy this test.

12. Given that the Supreme Court is extremely unlikely to revise its decision in X, I do not propose to examine the reasoning of the individual judges but rather will focus on the legal implications of the judgments as I understand them.

court. In *X* one of the material facts was that, in order to save the mother's life, there was no immediate alternative to termination of the pregnancy. The situation would be quite different if the foetus had developed to the point where it was, or would soon be, viable outside the womb. In this case it would be possible to vindicate both the life of the mother and that of the foetus by inducing labour or performing a caesarian section and it is simply absurd to think that *X* permits an abortion at that point.[13]

In my view, the Constitution does not preclude the introduction of time limits restricting the availability of abortion and this is an appropriate matter for the Oireachtas to determine.

Legislation will also be required to deal with other matters thrown up by the judgments in *X*. Some statutory regulation of the cogency of evidence necessary to justify an abortion is required as is statutory protection for the rights of those hospital personnel who do not wish, for religious or moral reasons, to assist in the termination of a pregnancy.

Deciding whether there is a real and substantial risk to the life of the mother is a matter of judgment in respect of which, one imagines, there is always room for debate. This is particularly so where the risk to life is a threat of suicide. However before one rejects the position reached in *X* because of the practical problems of application, it is necessary to consider what the alternatives are. Any restrictive modification of the majority judgments may involve acceptance of the proposition that, in some circumstances at least, the right to life of the foetus should prevail over the right to life of the mother.[14]

European Convention on Human Rights

The issue of abortion has come before the European Commission of Human Rights on only two occasions and it has yet to come before the Court of Human Rights.[15] Thus far, the decisions of the

---

13. Thus Mr Justice McCarthy says, '[T]he right of the unborn is to a life contingent; contingent on survival in the womb until successful delivery.'

14. There is one interesting jurisprudential problem which may arise in the event of there being any modification to Art.40.3.3. It is arguable that this constitutional provision recognises, rather than constitutes, a pre-existing right to life inhering in the unborn and in the mother. If this is so, and if the right to life is derived from an extra-constitutional source such as natural law, can the right be modified by positive law in the shape of a referendum?

15. For an examination of this area, see van Dijk and van Hoof, *Theory and Practice of the European Convention on Human Rights*, (2nd ed., 1990) at pp. 218-220.

Commission would appear to be characterised by a desire to avoid hard and fast rulings on this complicated question. In *Bruggeman and Scheuten v. Germany*[16] the Commission left open the question as to whether the foetus was covered by art.2 of the Convention which protects the right to life. In *X v. U.K.*[17] the Commission agreed that the foetus did not have an unqualified right to life under art.2 but did not feel it necessary to decide whether the foetus was totally excluded from the scope of that article or whether it had rights which must be balanced against those of the mother in a reasonable manner. As for arguments predicated on the mother's right to privacy, in *Bruggeman and Scheuten* the Commission held that laws of what was then West Germany, which permitted abortion only in the case of danger to the mother's life, health (physical or mental) or on eugenic grounds did not infringe the guarantee of privacy in art.8. It should be noted that, while these laws permit abortion on broader grounds than are allowed in *X*, it does not follow that the more restrictive Irish policy is necessarily contrary to the Convention.[18]

EC Law

Finally we turn to EC law. It is one of the ironies in the present situation that, while much of what was done was motivated by a desire to prevent the EC ever foisting an abortion policy on Ireland, there does not appear to be any evidence that harmonisation of abortion laws is on the Community's agenda. Following a careful and very thorough analysis of the possible legal bases in the Treaty of Rome or the jurisprudence of the Court of Justice for any such putative harmonisation policy, Kingston and Whelan conclude that the development of such a policy is 'perhaps possible, but not at all probable.'

This general view is also shared by Curtin who writes:

> [T]here is no possibility whatsoever of the Community legislature (or indeed the Court of Justice in Luxembourg) acting to legalise abortion itself *in Ireland*. The question of whether abortion should be legal or otherwise in a given member state is a

16. (1978) 10 D and R 100.
17. (1980) 19 D and R 244.
18. Kingston and Whelan, *loc. cit.* comment that 'the European Convention on Human Rights does not appear to envisage a *right* to abortion (although it *permits* it in at least some circumstances, which is not at all the same thing.)'

moral value judgment outside the scope of Community law and within the sphere of sovereign decision-making by member states.[19]

Thus it would appear that the threat of the EC coercing us into adopting a liberal abortion policy is more apparent than real. In any event, adoption of the Maastricht Protocol would head off even this perceived threat as its effect in this context would be to restrict the availability of abortions in Ireland to those permitted under art.40.3.3, thus arguably copperfastening X.

Of course, for those who wish to modify X, the Protocol may present a problem. If the Protocol is adopted by all of the member States of the Community, can Ireland subsequently amend the terms of art.40.3.3 unilaterally? In the absence of judicial authority, it is difficult to be dogmatic on the matter. However there is at least an argument that the other member States are entitled to assume that the reference to art.40.3.3 in the Protocol is a reference to that provision as it stood on 7 February 1992, the date on which the Maastricht Treaty was signed.[20]

This issue is addressed by the Solemn Declaration which indicates that the other Member States would look favourably on an amendment of the Protocol to incorporate a future constitutional amendment in Ireland concerning the subject matter of Art.40.3.3 'which does not conflict with the intention of the High Contracting Parties hereinbefore expressed'. It is difficult to know how far this takes us as the general view would appear to be that this Solemn Declaration is not legally binding and that it can, at most, only amount to a statement of political intent.[21] At the same time it is perhaps worth noting two points about the Solemn Declaration. First, it implies that a future amendment to the Constitution will not be covered by the terms of the Protocol, and thus immune from the effect of EC law, unless the other member States agree to amend that Protocol. Second, it implies that that approval will only be forthcoming for an amendment which does not conflict with freedom to travel or to receive and disseminate information under EC law.

19. *The Irish Times*, 2 March 1992.
20. See Callan, *The Sunday Tribune*, 19 April 1992.
21. Hogan, *The Irish Times*, 17-18 April 1992, Callan, *The Sunday Tribune*, 19 April 1992, Curtin, *The Irish Times*, 24 April 1992, Gwynn-Morgan, 27 April 1992.

THE RIGHT TO TRAVEL

National Law

The right to travel was first recognised as an implied constitutional right in *The State (M.) v. Attorney General*.[22] In *X*, three of the Supreme Court judges indicated, albeit in *obiter dicta*,[23] that the State could restrain a pregnant woman whose life was not endangered by the pregnancy from travelling abroad to obtain an abortion.[24] Unlike Mr Justice Costello in the High Court, however, none of these judges considered the impact of EC law on this aspect of domestic law which, given the fundamental importance, under EC law, of freedom to travel, does leave the majority analysis somewhat incomplete.

European Convention on Human Rights

By virtue of art.2(2) of the Fourth Protocol to the Convention, an individual has the right to leave his/her own country. This right may, however, be restricted on the grounds, *inter alia*, of public order or policy, of protecting health and morals, or of protecting the rights and freedom of others. There is very little case-law on this aspect of the Convention and it has been suggested that the right to leave is quite a weak one.[25]

EC Law

The position under EC law is quite different.[26] Free movement of persons is one of the cornerstones of the common market and is provided for under three different sets of provisions in the Treaty of Rome. Article 48 guarantees free movement within the Community for workers; art.52 provides, *inter alia*, that self-em-

---

22. [1979] I.R. 73.

23. *Obiter dicta* are statements made by a judge on a matter which s/he does not have to decide on the facts of the case before the court. As such they are not binding in subsequent cases, though they may have strong persuasive value. In the present case, the majority in the Supreme Court based their decision to lift the injunction on the need to protect the mother's right to life, rather than on any right to travel.

24. The two remaining judges, Mr Justices McCarthy and O'Flaherty took the contrary view, arguing that the State could not prevent a person travelling abroad in the circumstances of the *X* case.

25. van Dijk and van Hoof, *op. cit.* p.491.

26. For a clear account of EC law relating to freedom of movement, see the comment by Curtin in *The Irish Times*, 14 February 1992. See also *Mobility of People in the European Community* (Irish Centre for European Law, 1990).

ployed persons can pursue activities in other member States, while arts.59 and 60 provide for the free movement of persons providing services within the meaning of the Treaty. The latter two articles are relevant to our discussion of abortion. The case-law of the Court of Justice establishes that potential recipients of services are entitled to the benefit of arts.59 and 60 and in the recent case of *SPUC (Ireland) Ltd v. Grogan*[27] the Court of Justice held that the provision of abortion is a service for the purpose of those articles. Consequently it follows that a pregnant woman has a right under EC law to travel to another member State in order to avail of abortion services lawfully provided in that other country.[28]

In the absence of any amendment to EC law, therefore, it would appear that the State could not lawfully prevent a pregnant woman from travelling abroad in order to obtain an abortion.

This leads us on to one of the most hotly debated aspects of this entire debate – to what extent, if at all, does the Maastricht Protocol amend EC law in this regard in so far as such law applies to Ireland?[29] It will be recalled that this Protocol effectively provides that nothing in EC law shall affect the 'application in Ireland of Article 40.3.3 of the Constitution of Ireland.' Essentially this should protect certain steps taken under art.40.3.3 from being overturned by EC law.

There are now two diametrically opposed views as to what this means for the right to travel. On the one hand, it is argued that the words 'in Ireland' mean that the Protocol does not protect from EC law any activity having a transborder dimension. Conse-

27. [1991] 62 C.M.L.R. 849.

28. Mr Justice Costello's view that X's freedom to travel under EC law could be restricted by considerations of public policy has come in for criticism on the basis that such considerations have only ever been allowed to justify restrictions on persons coming into a country – they have never been used to restrict the freedom of people who wish to leave the jurisdiction – see separate comments by Curtin and Hogan in *The Irish Times*, 19 February 1992. It has also been suggested that the travel ban falls foul of EC law on the grounds that it is disproportionate to the objective which it seeks to achieve – see Hogan, *The Irish Times*, 24 February 1992, and Whelan, *The Irish Times*, 26 February 1992.

29. Curtin has suggested the possibility that the Court of Justice might yet find that the Protocol was not a valid exercise of inter-governmental rights because it trenched on fundamental rights and freedoms under EC law – *The Irish Times*, 7 March 1992. Hogan, however, while not entirely dismissive of this type of argument, describes it as 'radical', akin to the Irish courts holding that part of the Constitution is itself unconstitutional. For the purposes of this paper, I will assume that the Protocol is not itself invalid.

quently the existing right to travel to another member State in the EC is not affected by the Protocol.[30] On the other hand, it is contended that a majority of the judges in *X* indicated, albeit in *obiter dicta*, that art.40.3.3 permitted the State to restrict a woman from travelling abroad; that this was an interpretation of the 'application in Ireland' of that provision and that, consequently, this position would be copperfastened if the Protocol becomes law.[31]

The government's position on this argument would appear to be inconsistent inasmuch as the attempt to persuade the other member States to accept a modification to the Protocol was arguably premised on the belief that the Protocol, as it stood, did affect rights to travel and to receive and obtain information. However in the aftermath of the failure of that attempt, the government now suggests that the Protocol actually confirms the right to travel for Irish women.[32] This is expressly stated in the Solemn Declaration which purportedly[33] records the intention of the High Contracting Parties to the Maastricht Treaty that the Protocol should not limit, *inter alia*, freedom to travel within the Community. However it is generally agreed that the Solemn Declaration has no legal effect and that it can, at most, only amount to a declaration of political intent.[34]

The assurance from the Attorney General that the effect of a 'yes' vote to Maastricht on 18 June would thereafter preclude him from obtaining an injunction to restrain a woman from travelling

30. See Binchy, *The Irish Times*, 25 February 1992, 27 February 1992, Curtin, *The Irish Times*, 2 March 1992, 7 March 1992, 24 April 1992. See also the reported views of 'senior legal experts' at the Court of Justice in Luxembourg in *The Irish Times*, 25 February 1992.
31. See Hogan, *The Irish Times*, 24 February 1992, 6 March 1992, 17-18 April 1992, 25 April 1992, McDowell, *The Irish Times* 6 March 1992.
32. See the government White Paper on the Maastricht Treaty, published 23 April 1992.
33. It has been pointed out that the signatories of the Solemn Declaration, the Foreign Ministers of the member States are not, in fact, the High Contracting Parties to the Maastricht Treaty, who are the member States themselves and who will decide on ratification through their parliaments or people as the case may be – Callan, *The Sunday Tribune*, 19 April 1992. The point has also been made that if the Solemn Declaration is an accurate account of the intention of the Irish government when it signed the Treaty and Protocol on 7 February 1992, then the action of the Attorney General on the previous day in commencing proceedings for an injunction to restrain X from travelling flew in the face of this understanding of the Protocol – see McDowell, *The Irish Times*, 17-18 April 1992. See also the reported comments of Hogan in *The Irish Times*, 2 May 1992.
34. See references at footnote 21 above.

abroad is also not without difficulty and has been trenchantly criticised.[35]

Much of this criticism would appear to arise from a misunderstanding of the Attorney General's arguments. The criticism arguably assumes that the assurance is based on the view that the vote on 18 June would create a new legal norm on the right to travel altering the position which is generally understood to obtain in the aftermath of X (i.e. that the right to travel may be restricted in order to protect the right to life of the unborn). If the assurance was based on such a view, then indeed it would be difficult to defend. The vote on 18 June of itself does not create any new legal norms as the Maastricht Treaty must also be ratified by the other member States and cannot come into effect any earlier than 1 January 1993; as we have seen above, it is by no means clear that the Protocol will leave intact the EC right to travel; finally, the Solemn Declaration is not legally binding.

However all this arguably misreads the Attorney General's position. As I understand it, his assurance is based on the view that a 'yes' vote to the Protocol would be to the Protocol as interpreted in the Solemn Declaration[36] and that such a vote would be evidence that public policy as expressed by the people in a referendum does not contemplate interference with a right to travel in order to vindicate the right to life of the unborn. Thus he is not arguing that a new norm will come into existence on 18 June; rather he contends that we will have new evidence which will influence our interpretation of the existing norm in art.40.3.3. The construction of the Constitution in the light of public opinion is certainly an acceptable method of constitutional interpretation[37] and thus the Attorney General's views cannot be dismissed completely out of hand.

---

35. See Hogan, *The Irish Times*, 25 April 1992. See also his reported comments in *The Irish Times*, 2 May 1992.

36. That the Solemn Declaration might arguably misrepresent the original intention of the High Contracting Parties when they signed the Maastricht Treaty, including the Protocol, does not, it would seem to me, affect the Attorney General's argument. As I understand it, he contends that a 'yes' vote on 18 June would amount to an endorsement, by the People, of the public policy described in the Solemn Declaration, which view of public policy could then be used to construe art.40.3.3.

37. Sometimes referred to as the 'historical approach' to constitutional interpretation.

At the same time, there are difficulties with his position. In the first place, this would appear to be a very convoluted way of amending the Constitution, one which undermines the terms of art.47 of the Constitution (which provides for amendment of the Constitution by way of referendum following the enactment of appropriate legislation). Second, if the Attorney General is correct, then one wonders why is it necessary to have a further referendum on the right to travel and to information next November?

Perhaps the only point clear from all of the foregoing is that there is no unanimity among lawyers as to the effect, in Irish law, of the Protocol to the Maastricht Treaty. The short answer to someone seeking authoritative guidance as to the effect of this Protocol on the right to travel is that we will have to await a decision of the Court of Justice on the matter. However if I was pushed to choose between the conflicting opinions on this matter, then, taking into account the history of the Court of Justice in promoting the supremacy of EC law and its uniform application in all member States, I would think it slightly more probable that that Court would construe the Protocol so as to preserve intact the right of Irish citizens under EC law to travel abroad in order to obtain lawful services.

THE RIGHT TO INFORMATION

National Law

Prior to the decision in *X*, the only aspect of art.40.3.3 which had been considered by the Irish courts was its impact on the dissemination of abortion information. In *Attorney General (SPUC (Ireland) Ltd) v. Open Door Counselling Ltd*[38] the Supreme Court granted an injunction restraining the defendants from 'assisting pregnant women within the jurisdiction to travel abroad to obtan abortions by referral to a clinic; by the making of their travel arrangements, or by informing them of the identity and location of and method of communication with a specified clinic or clinics'. The right of private organisations such as SPUC to seek such injunctions was subsequently upheld in *SPUC (Ireland) Ltd v. Grogan*.[39]

The issue of access to abortion information did not arise in *X* and was commented on by only one of the Supreme Court judges

38. [1988] I.R. 593.
39. [1989] I.R. 753.

– Mr Justice O'Flaherty cited the *Open Door* case as authority for the proposition that '[p]romotional propaganda in respect of abortions abroad is prohibited.' Nonetheless it is unarguable that the absolute ban on the dissemination of abortion information cannot stand in the light of *X*, if only insofar as that a woman whose life is endangered by a pregnancy is entitled to such information in order to vindicate her own right to life.[40] Precisely how the dissemination of information in such a case should be organised is really an appropriate matter for the Oireachtas to resolve. Should it be felt desirable to make abortion information available on a wider basis, an amendment to the Constitution would be required, and indeed, such is promised for next November.[41]

Both the *Open Door* and *Grogan* cases have been appealed to Europe, to the European Court of Human Rights and the Court of Justice respectively, and it is to these that I now turn.

European Convention on Human Rights

As I have already mentioned,[42] the initial stage of a complaint alleging infringement of the Convention is handled by the European Commission on Human Rights. In its report published on 7 March 1991, the Commission held, by a majority of eight to five, that Irish law violated art.10 of the Convention, guaranteeing freedom of expression, because the activities of the defendants were not proscribed by law, the terms of art.40.3.3 being insufficiently precise for this purpose and there being an absence of any legislation or relevant, well-established case-law on the matter. Three of the majority Commissioners also indicated that the Irish measures went beyond what was necessary in a democratic society because they were disproportionate. In this context, it was noted that a ban on information was ineffective in protecting the right to life of the unborn in the absence of a ban on travel.

The case was argued before the Court of Human Rights on 24 March 1992 at which stage, counsel for the State conceded that the limited right to abortion recognised in the *X* case meant that women were also now entitled to abortion information in certain

---

40. This was accepted by counsel for the State in argument before the European Court of Human Rights in the *Open Door* case on 24 March 1992.
41. An important question here, of course, is whether an information ban is effective in vindicating the right to life of the unborn. In *Open Door* three members of the European Commission on Human Rights took the view that it is not.
42. See footnote 4.

limited circumstances. A decision from the Court is expected later this year.

In the event of the Court upholding the ban on information, which is no longer absolute in the light of the State's concession, then clearly there will be no change in what is currently understood to be the position under domestic law. Some legislation will be required in order to regulate the provision of abortion information to those women whose lives are endangered by their pregnancies. But should the Court follow the lead of the Commission, then, as Kingston and Whelan point out,

[t]he Government [will be] in something of a quandary. If it wishes to restrict information on the availability of information on abortion outside the jurisdiction, it must do so on the basis of clear legislation; such legislation must also be effective; to be effective, to prevent the destruction of foetal life, it must presumably be coupled with an enforceable ban on travel.... However if such [a measure is] taken ... the issue of violation of other Convention rights, *inter alia*, privacy (article 8), liberty (article 5) and freedom from inhuman and degrading treatment (article 3) may also arise. However, failure to restrict information (and possibly travel) may result in a failure to comply with article 40.3.3. The question then arises as to whether article 40.3.3, as interpreted at present, can ever be compatible with the Convention.

EC Law

The day before the European Commission on Human Rights published its report in the *Open Door* litigation, the Court of Justice heard argument in *SPUC (Ireland) Ltd v. Grogan*.[43] The Court had been asked, first to decide whether the medical termination of pregnancy came within the definition of 'services' for the purposes of art.60 of the Treaty of Rome, second, whether a member State could prohibit the distribution of information about abortion services in another member State and, finally, whether there existed a Community law right to distribute, in a member State, information about abortion facilities abroad if abortion is prohibited under the laws of that member State.

The Court answered the first question in the affirmative. In re-

43. [1991] 62 C.M.L.R. 849.

lation to the second and third questions, it held that it was not contrary to Community law for a member State in which abortion is forbidden to prohibit the distribution of information about abortion facilities abroad where the agencies providing such facilities have no involvement in the distribution of the information. In the present case, that meant that SPUC could obtain an injunction against various students' unions in Ireland restraining such bodies from distributing information about abortion facilities in the U.K.

However the clear implication of this ruling is that one may not be entitled to prevent an abortion clinic operating elsewhere in the EC from advertising its services in Ireland.

How will this situation be affected if the Protocol is adopted? Again we are back to the debate which we first encountered in the context of the right to travel. On one view, a ban on abortion information represents the 'application in Ireland' of art.40.3.3 and consequently will be rendered immune from challenge under EC law if the Protocol is approved. On the other hand, one could argue that the dissemination of information about abortion services abroad has a trans-border element which takes it outside the scope of the Protocol.

The Solemn Declaration, meanwhile, indicates that the High Contracting Parties did not consider the Protocol to affect the freedom to obtain or make available in Ireland information relating to services lawfully available in other member States.[44] It further recognises that this freedom may be made subject to conditions, prescribed by Irish legislation, which conform with EC law.

NOTHING DOGMATIC

It is unlikely that any other judicial decision in Irish history has generated as much public interest and controversy as *Attorney General v. X*. When the dust settles, this case will be seen as raising many interesting points about law and society. Few cases illustrate so dramatically the extent of the judicial power to interpret.

The case also provides food for thought on the appropriateness of using the Constitution to deal with a complex matter such as

---

44. This is very difficult to reconcile with the actual history of events as it would appear that the Protocol was sought by the government in order to neutralise the right to disseminate information implicit in the *Grogan* case. See also footnote 33 above.

abortion and, indeed, on the larger question of the efficacy of the law in enforcing morality.

In the short term, however, many people are seeking answers to the immediate legal questions which have arisen. More specifically, they wish to know what legal consequences attach to approval of the Maastricht Protocol. The short answer to this question is that it is impossible to be authoritative about the meaning of this text. As we have seen, the following legal views have been expressed about the Protocol – that it may be invalid as an infringement of fundamental rights under EC law; that it will be interpreted narrowly by the Court of Justice so as to preserve the existing rights of Irish people under EC law to travel and to obtain information about abortion services available abroad; that it will copperfasten X, on the one hand removing EC rights to travel and to information and on the other preventing any modification of the the Supreme Court's judgment on the substantive issue of abortion. In the absence of an authoritative interpretation of the Protocol by the Court of Justice it is simply impossible to give an assured answer as to which and how many of these views are correct.

Given the absence of any one obvious meaning of the text of the Protocol, it seems to me that policy considerations may prove decisive in determining how it will be construed by the Court of Justice. Consequently I incline, very tentatively, to the view that the Protocol may be interpreted so as to preserve existing rights to travel and information. This approach may also colour the Community's attitude to any future attempt to modify the law on what is now being referred to as the 'substantive' issue of abortion – in other words, provided such modification does not affect transborder rights such as the right to travel and the right to information, the EC will not get involved.

However, one lesson which we should all have learnt from recent events is that, in this area at least, it is impossible to be dogmatic.

POSTSCRIPT

Mr Eoghan Fitzsimons has suggested that the paragraph in the Solemn Declaration dealing with the legal interpretation of the Protocol is in fact legally binding (*Irish Times*, 6 May 1992). This opinion appeared too late for consideration here.

European Dimensions of the Abortion Debate

WILLIAM ROBINSON

Cultural, religious and moral diversity between the Member States of the European Communities make for obstacles to the effectiveness of community law in achieving 'an ever closer union among the peoples of Europe' as envisaged by all the Treaties furthering the integration of the European Communities. The principle of the effectiveness of Community Law, as one of the policy objectives of the Court of Justice of the European Communities, has required its uniform application and interpretation throughout the Community.

The issue of abortion focuses moral, ethical and legal debate. The addition of the (historically) economically based law of the European Communities has further complicated the debate, by casting doubts upon rights enshrined in the Irish Constitution. The dramatic timing of developments in this field has called into question the ability of the Member States of the European Community to ratify the Treaty on European Union without subjecting themselves to a unified moral code. However, the goal of European Union requires that problems arising from the diversity of cultures be addressed in the process of integration itself. The jurisprudence of the Court of Justice does, and must, therefore encompass non-economically related values, such as the notion of Union Citizenship in the Treaty of European Union, if it is to establish an unwritten constitutional charter for European Union.

CHRONOLOGY

Up to this year the cases brought under Article 40.3.3 of the Irish Constitution (the 'pro-life' amendment) have concerned the provision of information and advice in Ireland, and have not directly referred to the unenumerated right to travel in the Constitution of Ireland. The Society for the Protection of Unborn Children (SPUC) sought and obtained an injunction in 1988 against two organisations based in Dublin, Open Door Counselling and the Dublin Well-Woman Centre. The organisations supplied 'non-directive' counselling to women, and if the woman decided upon an abortion, would provide them with names, addresses and telephone numbers of clinics in the United Kingdom, as well as assisting in the organisation of travel arrangements. The injunction was upheld in the Supreme Court.[1] Chief Justice Finlay believed that no reference was necessary to the Court of Justice of the European communities. SPUC then sought to apply the injunction to three students' unions which were distributing similar information to its members. The High Court in this case, *SPUC -v- Grogan*, referred three question to the Court of Justice of the European Communities.

The Court of Justice, however, avoided addressing the central issues by relying on the lack of an economic link between the students' unions and the clinics.[2] The Court of Justice answered the first question on whether the termination of pregnancy could constitute a 'service', but declined to answer the remaining question, concerning the provision of information, on the ground that the economic nexus was 'too tenuous' to fall within the Treaty. The decision that it could not consider the matter was partially motivated by the fact that a review of the Supreme Court's ruling in the *Open Doors Counselling* case was pending before the European Commission and Court of Human Rights. In the absence of a Court of Justice ruling, an opinion on the state of Community law in that case was expressed by Advocate General Van Gerven.[3] The Advocate General reached the same conclusion as the Irish Supreme Court, although based on different reasoning.

The Irish Government, as a reaction to the *Grogan* case and, presumably, the Opinion of the Advocate General, attempted to protect the right to life of the unborn child in the Treaty on European Union, agreed at Maastricht on 9 and 10 December 1991, by promoting the insertion of a Protocol, little-noticed at the time by Community specialists, which provided that 'Nothing in the Treaty on the European Union, or in the Treaties establishing the European Communities, or in the Treaties or Acts modifying or supplementing those Treaties, shall affect the application in Ireland or Article 40.3.3 of the Constitution of Ireland.

1. [1988] 2 C.M.L.R. 443
2. Case C-159/90 [1991] 3 C.M.L.R. 849
3. Although Advocate General's Opinions are not binding on the Court of Justice, they are of persuasive authority, and have recently been cited by the Court in its judgments.

Prior to the insertion of the Protocol, case-law as to the extent of Article 40.3.3 was inconclusive. The position was complicated by the Supreme Court decision in *Attorney-General -v-. X.* Three judges (Finlay C.J., Hederman and Egan JJ.) believed the un-enumerated right to could travel could, as a matter of pure national law, be restricted by Article 40.3.3.

This interpretation of Article 40.3.3 directly contradicted the Opinion of Advocate Van Gerven concerning the fundamental Community law right to freedom of movement to receive services, and the Irish government's own submission in the *Grogan* case.

The new Taoiseach, Albert Reynolds, proposed an amendment to the Protocol in order to re-establish his Govenment's policy position. However, due to the number of Member States with second thoughts about the Treaty, the Council refused the request to amend the Protocol. The Irish government has therefore proposed to clarify the Protocol by means of a Solemn Declaration by the High Contracting States, which states 'that it was and is their [the High Contracting Parties] intention that the protocol shall not limit freedom either to travel between Member States or, in accordance with conditions which may be laid down, in conformity with Community Law, by Irish legislation, to obtain or make available in Ireland information relating to services lawfully available in Member States.'

The Solemn Declaration attempts to clarify the extent of the derogation from Community law provided in the Protocol. Its aim is to restore to the jurisdiction of Community law issues which, under the Protocol, would have been a matter for the interpretation of Irish Courts under Article 40.3.3. The Solemn Declaration re-establishes, in particular, the Government's policy position, as submitted to the Court of Justice in *Grogan* and at the negotiations at Maastricht, in relation to the freedom of movement to receive services where legally provided in other Member States.

ABORTION, INFORMATION AND SERVICES

Before *Grogan*, the Court of Justice had developed the right of freedom of movement to receive services as a necessary corollary to the freedom to 'receive' services provided for in Article 59 of the Treaty of Rome. Whilst expanding this right, in *Luisi and Carbone*,[4] the Court expressly included the provision of medical

4. Joined Cases 286/82 and 26/83 [1984] E.C.R. 377

services. Although Mr Justice Walsh, Ireland's foremost human rights lawyer, and academic lawyers such as J. Weiler argued strongly that the destruction of a human life, by the act of abortion, could not by its very nature be classified as a service, these arguments were dismissed by the Court of Justice in *Grogan*. The Court of Justice ruled that

> whatever the merits of those arguments on a moral plane ... medical termination of pregnancy, performed in accordance with the law of the State in which it is carried out, constitutes a service within the meaning of Article 60 EEC.[5]

In *Grogan*, the Court of Justice did not address the corollary economic right of freedom to receive information, although the Advocate General was of the opinion that as the freedom to provide and receive service is a fundamental principle of the Treaty, it must be given 'the most extensive possible effectiveness'. The Advocate General believed that this included

> the right to receive, unimpeded, information in one's own member-State about providers of services in the other member-State and about how to communicate with them.[6]

Thus, the Court of Justice and the Advocate General have recognised broad economic rights in relation to abortion. The Treaties provided methods of derogating from the application of the fundamental economic principles of the Community. Article 56(1) – concerning the freedom to receive services – provides derogations on grounds of public policy, public security or public health, which differs only marginally from the derogations available to the freedom of movement of goods and persons.

The Court of Justice has also required that any national measure must be proportional to the aim to be achieved. Advocate General Van Gerven was of the opinion that a prohibition on travel to another Member State would be disproportionate, thereby indicating that the Supreme Court's interpretation of Article 40.3.3. in *Attorney-General -v- X* regarding the curtailment of right to travel was contrary to Community law. However, he considered that the prohibition on the provision of information in Ireland which would 'assist' persons travelling to another Member

---

5. [1991] 3 C.M.L.R 849 at paras. 20 and 21
6. [1991] 3 C.M.L.R. 849 Opinion at para. 18

State was proportional. Thus he achieved the same result as the Supreme Court, in *Open Doors Counselling*, although from the opposite direction of argument.

The Court of Justice did not seize upon the opportunity to develop a line of case-law analogous to that developed in relation to the free movement of goods. Although national measures which prohibit freedom of movement could not benefit from the Treaty's derogations, as in Article 56(1), the Court has held that they will not fall within the prohibition itself, if they constitute a mandatory requirement of the Member State and are proportional to their aim. The court has held that matters such as 'Sunday trading' and the protection of the national film industry would thus fall outside the prohibition on obstacles to the free movement of goods on the grounds of 'political and economic choices'. The Court of Justice, by not addressing these economic principles, was also able to circumvent discussion on whether or not the prohibition of information breached the general principles of Community Law, which include human rights.

HUMAN RIGHTS

The Court of Justice has established through a series of cases that the protection of fundamental rights and freedoms, in particular those enshrined in the European Convention on Human Rights (ECHR), is an integral part of the general principles of Community law. Should an interpretation of an abortion issue become necessary, a conflict between the fundamental principles of the Constitution of Ireland and those of Community law may arise. The consequence of Article 29 of the Irish Constitution is that the European Convention on Human Rights has no domestic effect in Ireland. Although Mr Justice Walsh has argued strongly against the importation of the case-law of the European Court of Human Rights into domestic law, via Community law as being contrary to the objectives of the European Communities, the transformation to a European Union erodes reliance upon Article 29.

The restrictions granted under Article 40.3.3. on information, for the protection of the unborn child, may potentially, and in the Court of Justice's case-law, must, be considered in the light of the Commission of Human Rights' Report[7] of 7 March 1991, in which, by eight votes to five, it ruled that there has been a breach of Arti-

7. See 12 H.R.L.J. (1991) p 479

cle 10 ECHR, on freedom of expression, in respect of the Supreme Court's ruling int he *Open Door Counselling* case. The matter is currently before the European Court of Human Rights.[8]

In *Grogan*, Advocate General Van Gerven believed that conflicts between fundamental human rights, as enshrined in the general principles of Community Law, and the Constitution of Ireland, should be balanced in a manner 'analogous to the principle of proportionality used in the Community'. However, the development of the principles of supremacy of Community law led, in the case of *Elliniki Radiophonia-Teleorasi v. Dimotiki Etairia Pliroforissis*,[9] to the direct testing by the Court of Justice of the compatibility of national legislation with the protection of human rights laid down in Community law. In this process the Court of Justice displaces the supreme national constitutional court as the final arbiter, in the Community system, of the legitimacy of laws having regard to the principles of human rights. The human rights argument illustrates the potential differences between purely economic reasoning and the belief in fundamental moral or cultural rights. The Court of Justice may therefore be faced with critical choices between attempting to enforce moral code throughout Europe and accepting the limits on the potential effectiveness and uniformity of Community law.

ISSUES ARISING

The problem of national cultural and moral diversity is not new to the Community. The case of *Groener*[10] also involved a problem arising from Ireland's cultural diversity. Ms Groener, a Dutch woman, was refused a teaching position in Ireland on the ground that she could not speak Gaelic. The Court of Justice held that the measure was not contrary to Community law, as it was a proportional and non-discriminatory 'means of expressing national identity and culture', which was enshrined in the Constitution. The incorporation in the Treaty on European Union of a proliferation of Protocols and agreements which attempt to solve such issues appears to indicate a dissatisfaction and lack of trust in the Community and the Court of Justice and their ability to resolve issues of similar diversity. The adoption of the Protocol and the Solemn

---

8. Oral Hearing, 23 March 1992
9. Case C-260/89 Judgement of 18 June 1991, not yet reported.
10. Case C-379/87 *Groener v. Minister of Education* [1989] E.C.R. 3967.

Declaration attempts to clarify the legal derogation required from the Treaties in respect of Irish national culture and moral identity, as articulated in Article 40.3.3.

However, the case-law addressed above indicates that the state of Community and Irish law was far from cler rboth before and after the negotiation of the Protocol and subsequent Solemn Declaration. There exist grounds for potential conflicts between the Treaty, the Protocol and the Solemn Declaration which requires an analysis of the legal status of the various provisions, and the nature of the principles which are in conflict. Such conflicts may arise in particular from the interpretation of Article 40.3.3. by the Irish Supreme Court and the status of the fundamental principles of both economic and human rights in Community law.

Legal status is governed by both public international law[11] and the Treaties establishing the European communities. Article 239 EEC provides that Protocols are an 'integral part' of the Treaty of Rome, and as such are fully binding on the Court of Justice. This status would therefore be similarly conferred upon the Protocol in question, if Article 239 applies *mutatis mutandis* to the Treaty on European Union. Should this not be so, international law provides that Protocols shall be fully binding if an integral part of[12] or in connection with the Treaty. It is likely therefore that the Protocols are fully binding on the Court of Justice. The Court of Justice may not strike down a Treaty provision or similar act (*Laisa v. Council*).

UNCLEAR STATUS OF SOLEMN DECLARATION

The Solemn Declaration by the High Contracting Parties is not, however, a Protocol but constitutes a statement of collective intention, initiated by Ireland. It must therefore be established whether the Solemn Declaration is of binding effect on the Court of Justice under international and/or Community law, or is of some lesser authority.

There exists no binding authority on the legal status of Declarations appended to Community Treaties, and opinions on the subject vary. It has never been assumed, for example, that the Solemn Declaration of Stuttgard of 19 June 1983, on European Union,

11. The Vienna Convention on the Law of Treaties of 1969.
12. *Ambatielos Case: Greece v. United Kingdom*, preliminary Objection, I.C.j. Rep. 1952 28

was legally binding. Similarly, the case law of the Court of Justice on the interpretation and status of declarations passed contemporaneously to secondary legislation, indicates, by analogy, that they are of no legal effect.[13] The legal effect of the Declaration is therefore unclear.

The issues of fundamental rights and moral diveristy within the Community may therefore re-appear, further complicated by the unclear legal effect of what were intended as clarifying provisions.

The problems caused by the uncertain legal effect of the Solemn Declaration, and to a lesser extent that of the Protocol, are further complicated by the nature of the principles which conflict. The Court of Justice, in its opinion on the draft agreement with the EFTA countries to form the European Economic Area (EEA), outlined the development of a hierarchy of norms within Community law.[14] In its Opinion the Court traced the development of free trade and economic principles beyond the words of the Treaties into a Community legal order, which had as its goal a European Union. As such, the Community was a constitutional charter based on the rule of law. The Court held that the European Economic Area Treaty was contrary to this new species of international entity. The Community has principles so fundamental to its existence that any alteration or dilution of these, as existed in the EEA Treaty would prohibit their enactment.

The potential development of a hierarchy of norms within Community law is further clarified by the Court's insistence upon classification of the free trade and economic rights as 'a means to an end'. If, therefore, unwritten elements of Community law, such as the protection of fundamental rights and freedoms, are part of the higher norm (and it is hard to see them in any other light), it must be questioned whether the adoption of the Protocol and Solemn Declaration of the issue of abortion can derogate from such a fundamental element of the Community constitution. The federalist vocation of the Court of Justice may partially explain the lack of trust being displayed by the Member States in their adoption of Protocols. However, the adoption of a hierarchy of norms by the Court of Justice would enable it to minimise the use of such political techniques.

---

13. *Regina v Immigration Appeal Tribunal, ex parte Antonissen* case C-292/89, judgement of 26 February 1991, not yet reported.

14. Opinion 1/91, not yet published.

CONCLUSION

The prospect of becoming so tantalisingly close to a Union without its final achievement epitomises the inherent difficulties in creating a federation in which the Member States have diverse cultural, religious and moral values. The Court of Justice, in attempting to incite and coax obedience from Member States, may, with the creation of an unwritten Community constitution with a hierarchy of norms, have combined principles which expose fundamental problems for individual Member States with particular cultural, religious and moral beliefs. The coherence of the Constitution of Ireland, the fundamental economic rights of Community law and human rights, as incorporated in the general principles of Community law, remains in flux.

Political compromises, both in respect of the abortion issues and the Protocol and agreement on Social Policy, have created innumerable legal problems and cast doubt upon the possibility of legally effective multi-speed integration. The ratification of the Maastricht Treaty, if achieved, will not therefore necessarily prevent the legal mine-field of derogations created by its provisions nor 'abortion tourism'.

Abortion Law: the Tragic Choices

SIMON LEE

Law has been used in Ireland, and elsewhere for that matter, as a false target for morality. Hack golfers who hook or slice simply set their sights on an imaginary target to the right or left, respectively, of the flag; that way, they think that they will end up more or less in the right direction. Similarly, if certain moralists want to end abortion they delude themselves into believing that if they aim for the false target of constitutional law they will reach their true moral destination, whether by political hook or – cynics would say – by episcopal crook.

For a time, this strategy can work, up to a point. But unless the root problem is addressed, the swing perfected and the aim straightened, only the appearance of progress can be made. It might be enough to fool those watching from afar who only see the confident walk down the moral fairway. The lie, however, is revealed to those who end up in the rough.

The 1983 anti-abortion amendment campaign focused on the false target of constitutional law, and another decade was lost in the task of getting the moral line straight. There is a danger in 1992 of history repeating itself.

DUBIOUS ARGUMENTS

Certainly, arguments in the forthcoming referenda will be repetitious. In what follows, I will try not to repeat myself. For my views, therefore, I would simply refer readers to my book, *Law and Morals*. Since writing that, however, I have been drawn into innumerable debates about such matters and I have come to the conclusion that all sides in such discussions rely far too much on bad arguments. As a minor contribution to the continuing debate in Ireland, I would like to begin by identifying what I would regard as these dubious modes of argument.

Campaigners, opinion-formers, and politicians engage in polarising rhetoric rather than genuine debate. What a beneficial change it would be if instead it was acknowledged that these issues present tragic choices between compelling arguments which are held on all sides in good faith.

There are five questionable lines of approach which I would like to see banished from all discussions of law and morals. The first type of attack is often name-calling: 'You would say that, wouldn't you, because you're a Catholic/a man/fertile/infertile/ a doctor/a research scientist'. I know that many consider at least the first two to be good arguments but I would prefer to consider the quality of the arguments rather than some aspects of the identity of the speaker.

A second trick is seeking to win the debate by definitions. All language is morally loaded (one campaigner's unborn child is another's clump of cells) but some is more loaded than others. On the one hand, there are scientists who are only too willing to call a spade a pre-spade. The term 'pre-embryo', for example, is now used by some researchers. It attracts support for the Warnock majority proposal by implying that the pre-fourteen-day embryo has an inferior moral worth to the post-fourteen-day embryo. These embryologists, who do not call themselves pre-embryologists, never used that term before the Warnock committee drew that line. On the other side, we hear the accusation that scientists are 'playing God'. But what exactly does this mean? This is a linguistic smoke-screen which obscures an absence of reasoning. Surely it is not the scientists who are guilty of *hubris* here but their accusers, in implying that humans could play God.

A third over-used technique is to pray in aid the so-called 'slippery slope' argument (sometimes called the 'domino effect'). The debating ploy is to say 'if you ban this hard core pornography today, then you will ban Shakespeare or Disney tomorrow'. The implication is that since it would be ridiculous to ban Shakespeare or Disney, we should not even set foot on the slippery slope of censorship by banning pornography, else we will slide down the hill to total censorship. Pro-lifers will claim that if we allow experiments *in invitro* embryos up to fourteen days, then next year it will be a month, then three months. Meanwhile, pro-choicers argue that if we restrict abortion to eighteen weeks, then next year it will be fifteen then twelve. The reality is that it is extraordinarily difficulty to get any change in these kinds of laws – as the last thirty years of procedural mugging by both sides shows in relation to abortion in Britain. Too often we are faced with clambering up the slippery slopes to the law more than sliding down them. We have to accept that the reality is that we are always already on the slope, holding a position. Most legal systems already allow abortion in some circumstances and prohibit it in others. Free speech is not absolute. Some expression is censored yet we do not necessarily slide down the slope towards more censorship. With the right equipment, we can maintain our foot-hold.

A fourth argument which I treat with suspicion is the claim that the law cannot stop abortion, pornography or whatever is under discussion, so why try? This is usually expressed in terms of pushing an activity underground (e.g. pornography) or into the back streets (e.g. abortion) or abroad (e.g. experiments on embryos). But the law does not stop all murder, yet most of us are grateful that it tries.

A fifth tactical move is the facile assertion that opponents are being inconsistent. There are two lines of rebuttal. One is to say that there are subtle differences which explain alleged inconsistencies, as for example between banning experiments altogether, or after fourteen days, yet allowing later abortions. Some people believe that the different intentions of the experimenter and the abortionist, or the different location of the embryo in a petri dish or in a woman's womb, are morally relevant factors. It behoves the sceptics among us to listen and argue rather than to whoop with delight at the superficial difficulties.

The other plausible strategy is to admit an inconsistency but to accept that the law should not necessarily be consistent across the range of tragic choices. Indeed, the only way in which a society can come to terms with its conflicting values is to prefer one value in some circumstances and another in different conditions. It is difficult enough for an individual, let alone a society to be consistent. Are all pro-lifers anti-capital punishment, anti-nuclear weapons and anti-cars (which inevitably cause some deaths)?

THE RIGHT TO LIFE OF THE UNBORN

Turning to the Irish law, the wording of the Eighth Amendment and the facts of *AG -v- X* are well-known but they do merit repetition:

> The State acknowledges the right to life of the unborn and, with due regard to the equal right to life of the mother, guarantees in its laws to respect, and, as far as practicable, by its laws to defend and vindicate that right.

A fourteen year old girl, X, became pregnant as the result of an alleged rape. Her parents took her to England for an abortion. They asked the gardaí whether genetic fingerprinting would assist a prosecution of the alleged rapist. The gardaí referred the issue of the admissibility of such evidence to the Director of Public Prosecutions who informed the Attorney General who obtained interim injunctions in the High Court to prevent the girl and her parents from procuring an abortion within or without the jurisdiction and indeed from leaving the jurisdiction for nine months. At the full hearing, a psychologist testified that there was a risk the girl might commit suicide as she had repeatedly threatened. Costello J. granted the permanent injunctions on the ground that Article 40.3.3. of the Constitution required him to balance the risk to life of the girl and her unborn child, that there was a real and imminent danger to the life of the unborn if he did not grant the injunctions but that the risk that X might take her own life if the injunctions were granted was of a less and different order of magnitude. Although the judge accepted that there was a *prima facie* right to travel to another member state to receive a service lawful in that state, under European Community Law, nonetheless the Eighth Amendment was a clear expression of public policy which would justify Ireland derogating from that right.

The Supreme Court soon heard an appeal in which counsel for the Attorney General conceded that part of the injunction was too broad (that which refrained X from leaving the jurisdiction for any purpose whatsoever) and that the Eighth Amendment envisaged lawful abortion in Ireland where (but only where) the mother's life was in imminent and inevitable danger of death. A four-to-one majority of the Supreme Court allowed the appeal and lifted the injunctions. The judges stopped the argument before the European Community points were reached and resolved the matter on the basis that abortion was lawful in Ireland where it was established as a matter of probability that there was a real and substantial risk to the life of the mother if such termination were not effected. The risks to the life of the mother included a real and substantial risk that she might commit suicide. Nonetheless, the majority of the court maintained that where there was not such a risk and where it would thus be unlawful to procure an abortion in Ireland, the courts could exercise their equitable discretion to restrain by injunction the removal of the unborn from the jurisdiction so as to be defend and vindicate the unborn's right to life.

SUICIDE THREATS

Like courts elsewhere, then, the Irish Supreme Court tried to decide the matter on the narrowest possible ground. Rather than even consider the European aspects of the case, the Court focused on the particular facts of suicidal threats.

Mr Justice Hederman, dissenting, argued that 'suicide threats can be contained. The duration of the pregnancy is a matter of months and it should not be impossible to guard the girl against self-destruction and preserve the life of the unborn child at the same time.... On the vital matter of the threat to the mother's life there has been a remarkable paucity of evidence.'

Other judges disagreed. Costello J. at first instance said:

> When the defendant learned that she was pregnant she naturally was greatly distraught and upset. Later she confided in her mother that when she learned she was pregnant she had wanted to kill herself by throwing herself downstairs. On the journey back from London she told her mother that she had wanted to throw herself under a train when she was in London, that she had put her parents through so much trouble she would rather be dead than continue as she was. On the 31st January, in the course of a long discussion with a member of the Garda Síochána, she said: 'I wish it were all over, sometimes I feel like throwing myself downstairs'. And in the presence of another member of the Garda Síochána, when her father commented that the 'situation was worse than a death in the family' she commented: 'Not if it was me'.

Chief Justice Finlay adopted those findings as fact and continued the story as follows in the Supreme Court:

> On the day of her return from London the defendant's parents brought her to a very experienced clinical psychologist. He explained in his report that he had been asked to assess her emotional state; that whilst she was co-operative she was emotionally withdrawn; that he had concluded that she was in a state of shock and that she had lost touch with her feelings. She told him that she had been crying on her own, but had hidden her feelings from her parents to protect them. His opinion was that her vacant expressionless manner indicated that she was cop-

ing with the appalling crisis she faced by a denial of her emotions. She did not seem depressed, but he said that she 'coldly expressed a desire to solve matters by ending her life'. In his opinion, in her withdrawn state, 'she was capable of such an act, not so much because she is depressed but because she could calculatingly reach the conclusion that death is the best solution'. He considered that the psychological damage to her of carrying a child would be considerable, and that the damage to her mental health would be devastating. His report was supplemented by oral testimony. He explained in the course of his consultation with the defendant she had said to him: 'It is hard at fourteen to go through the nine months' and that she had said: 'it is better to end it now than in nine months' time'. The psychologist understood this to mean that by ending her life she would end the problems through which she was putting her parents with whom she has a very strong and loving relationship.

The psychologist who gave oral evidence as well as submitting a report (which was admitted by agreement in evidence before the learned trial Judge) stated that when he had interviewed this young girl and was anxious to have a continuing discussion with her parents who accompanied her and not having anybody available to remain with the young girl in the waiting room, his view of the risk of her committing suicide was so real, on his past experience in this field of medicine, that notwithstanding its obvious inappropriateness he requested her to remain in the room while he discussed the problem with her parents.

Those who agree with the overall thrust of the majority seem to have adopted Mr Justice McCarthy's judgment as their favourite. On two points he wrote moving passages which deserve a wide circulation. Those obsessed with Anglo American jurisprudence and its rights talk, in particular, might appreciate the first. The judge said:

> I would prefer to seek harmony between the various rights guaranteed and to reconcile to each other rather than to rank one higher than another.... The right of the girl here is a right to life in being; the right of the unborn is to a life contingent; contingent on survival in the womb until successful delivery. It

is not a question of setting one above the other but rather of vindicating as far as practicable, the right to life of the girl/mother, whilst with due regard to the equal right to life of the girl/mother, vindicating, as far as practicable, the right to life of the unborn.... It is not a question of balancing the life of the unborn against the life of the mother; if it were the life of the unborn would virtually always have to be preserved, since the termination of pregnancy means the death of the unborn; there is no certainty, however high the probability, that the mother will die if there is not a termination of pregnancy. In my view, the true construction ... is that ... it is not a question of a risk of a different order of magnitude; it can never be otherwise than a risk of a different order of magnitude.

The second point on which the judge will be widely applauded was in his robust criticism of politicians' failure to follow up the Eighth Amendment with some detailed legislation:

I think it reasonable, however, to hold that the People when enacting the Amendment were entitled to believe that legislation would be introduced so as to regulate the manner in which the right to life of the unborn and the right to life of the mother could be reconciled. In the context of the eight years that have passed since the Amendment was adopted and the two years since Grogan's case the failure by the legislature to enact the appropriate legislation is no longer just unfortunate; it is inexcusable. What are pregnant women to do? What are the parent's of a pregnant girl under-age to do? What are the medical profession to do? They have no guidelines save what may be gleamed from the judgments in this case. What additional considerations are there? Is the victim of rape, statutory or otherwise, or the victim of incest, finding herself pregnant to be assessed in a manner different from others? The Amendment, born of public disquiet, historically divisive of our people, guaranteeing in its laws to respect and by its laws to defend the right to life of the unborn, remains bare of legislative direction.

Initially, the government seemed relieved that the girl in the particular case was free to travel and that the Supreme Court had not queered the pitch of the forthcoming Maastricht referendum by refusing to dabble in European matters. It soon became clear, however, that many problems remained. The pro-life lobby were appalled that abortion in these limited circumstances was now lawful within Ireland. Others were appalled that it was only available in these extremely rare circumstances. The lingering threat to the right to travel in other cases meant that a further problem arose concerning ratification of the Maastricht Treaty. The Irish Government had negotiated a protocol to the Treaty which reads:

> Nothing in the Treaty on the European union or in the Treaties establishing the European Communities or in the Treaties or Acts modifying or supplementing those Treaties shall affect the application in Ireland of Article 40.3.3 of the Constitution of Ireland.

It now seemed that the words 'application in Ireland' could be read as safeguarding the Irish Supreme Court's interpretation of Article 40.3.3. which, in effect, says that the application in Ireland extends to a prohibition on travel outside Ireland for the purposes of procuring an abortion. This would be unacceptable to the European Community in general, let alone to many Irish citizens, since it infringes a fundamental right to travel which (not withstanding the High Court judgment of Costello J.) European Community Law was unlikely to be prepared to see restricted. Meanwhile, the Irish Government was defending before the European Court of Human Rights at Strasbourg the earlier Supreme Court ruling which prohibited the provision of information about abortions lawfully available elsewhere.

IRISH LAW ON ABORTION: A BRIEF HISTORY

In order to understand the Irish law and its relationship to the law elsewhere in these islands, some summary of the common background and points of departure is necessary. On this issue, England, Northern Ireland and the Republic of Ireland start from a common foundation of the common law and a nineteenth century statute.

Before Parliament even existed, then, the common law prohibited abortion with some exceptions.

The 1861 Offences against the Person Act captures this by making it an offence to 'procure a miscarriage unlawfully'.

The next important stage in the story was the English case of *R. -v- Bourne*, a prosecution under section 58 of the Offences against the Person Act 1861. Dr Bourne's defence hinged on the word 'unlawfully'. The judge noted that long before the English parliament even came into existence, the killing of an unborn child was a grave crime under the common law of England. But he also noted that, as with the killing of an adult, there may be justification for the killing which the law might accept. It is this which was intended to be captured by the word 'unlawfully'.

Since counsel failed to cite helpful precedent, the judge turned to the Infant Life Preservation Act of 1929 because it, too, reflected that same attempt to express what had always been the common law. In 1929, parliament had chosen a fuller phrase than the word 'unlawfully' to convey the same idea. It had talked about acts (albeit in the context of the different offence of child destruction and a later stage of pregnancy) 'for the purpose only of preserving the life of the mother'.

What the judge suggested to the jury was that they needed to decide the meaning of the word 'unlawfully' in their statute but they might reflect on the phrase 'preserving the life of the mother' in the other statute as an attempt to grasp the same point. Then they might consider it difficult to distinguish between danger to the life and danger to the health of the mother.

Thus, we get to the point where he suggested they should acquit Dr Bourne if they felt that he honestly and reasonably believed that continuance of the pregnancy would make the girl in question 'a physical or mental wreck'.

Readers of John Keown's important book on abortion in England (*Abortion, Doctors and the Law*, Cambridge University Press, 1988) will know that it was really unnecessary for the judge to complicate matters by referring to the 1929 Act. There are cases before and after the 1861 Act in which judges were quite clear that there could be 'lawful cause' for procuring abortions. Keown observes that there was much extra-judicial authority for the same point and the only text book authority referred to during the trial, *Russell on Crime*, was equally clear that the word 'unlawfully' protected doctors who carried out an abortion in the interests even of the health of the mother, not just her life. Indeed, from this perspective, the judge's direction in *Bourne* has been described as more restrictive than the pre-existing law.

Whatever the merits or demerits of *Bourne* and however much it has been misunderstood, it seems an unsatisfactory way of leaving the law. As the summing-up in a trial, it was not even strictly binding in English, let alone Northern Irish, law. Although it undoubtedly has persuasive value, the time for legislation is long overdue.

The law in England was changed in 1967. What seems to have escaped the notice of many in the Irish debate is that in 1990, there were further amendments in the Human Fertilisation and Embryology Act. Neither of these two latest statutes apply to Northern Ireland but they leave the English law crystal clear, whether one likes it or not. But Northern Ireland is left with the task of interpreting the word 'unlawfully' in the 1861 statute. The South would be in the same position were it not for the Eighth Amendment and the Supreme Court's interpretation of it. For the moment, the Supreme Court has chosen an interpretation which seems narrower than *Bourne* and thus more restrictive than is the law in the North.

But in each legal system in Ireland, judges are trying to provide guidance on a tragic choice when legislators have failed to act. If the South now produces a coherent law on abortion, it will have leap-frogged the North where uncertainty looks set to remain.

NORTHERN IRELAND

Abortion in Northern Ireland is a twilight zone. Given the facts of *Bourne* or the current case (a fourteen-year-old alleged rape victim in both cases), an abortion would be lawful in Northern Ireland. But doctors are still left to gamble on defending themselves by reference to *Bourne*. Some assume that a modern judge would direct a jury to interpret 'unlawfully' in the 1861 Act even more broadly. Thus, abortions are regularly carried out here in cases of severe foetal handicap even though there appears to be no legal foundation for such terminations. Overall, about 500 abortions are performed annually in Northern Ireland, while more Northern Irish women seek terminations in Scotland or England.

Hence, the North faces a problem which the South and England thought they had avoided, namely, uncertainty. Decisions rest on the moral views and legal boldness of doctors who, thus, have too much power and too great a burden. The law could be clarified in any direction, permissive or restrictive of abortion, but it ought to be certain. This is a problem now shared by the South.

The Infant Life (Preservation) Act 1929 and its Northern Irish equivalent of 1945 dealt with a gap in the law where a child was, for example, deliberately strangled with the umbilical cord while being born. A defence could be made out to a charge of procuring a miscarriage that the child had already carried while against to a charge of murder or infanticide could rest on the claim that the child is not an independent being. After a well publicised acquittal in such a case, Parliament enacted, as ever, more speedily in England than in Northern Ireland.

TIME-LIMITS

The 1967 Act introduced four defences to a charge under the 1861 Act – Where the life of the mother, or her physical or mental health, or the physical and mental health of her children are at greater risk if the pregnancy continues than if it is terminated, and where there is a substantial risk of serious handicap. The 1967 Act referred to the 1929 legislation for a time limit thus giving a significance not originally intended to the rather lax drafting of the earlier statute such that the time limit became when the child is 'capable of being born alive' with a presumption that that happened after twenty-eight weeks.

This was seldom understood and for many years pro-lifers led a campaign to reduce the time limit to what, in legal reality, it already was! Thus, they talked as if the time limit were twenty-eight weeks and sought to reduce it e.g. to twenty-four. But given developments in technology such that foetuses could be delivered at twenty-four weeks the 1929 time limit self-adjusted.

A test case, *C. -v- S.*, showed the judges unwilling to interpret 'capable of being born alive' so as to reduce the time limit when Parliament was clearly unwilling to do so. The Master of the Rolls suggested that efforts to reform the law be directed to that body. So they were. Amendments to the Human Fertilisation and Embryology Act 1990 finally presented Parliament with the opportunity to reduce the time limit. In a spectacular farce, with MPs apparently not knowing what they were voting for (or against), this succeeded in 'reducing' the time limit to what it already was for some grounds, while removing it altogether for others and introducing the new ground! The new ground of 'grave permanent injury to the physical and mental health of the pregnant woman' is unlimited, as is 'the risk to life' and 'the substantial risk of serious handicap'. The other grounds run out at twenty-four weeks.

REPUBLIC OF IRELAND

The legal position in the South of Ireland would be the same as in the North (i.e. the 1861 Act applies as a pre-partition piece of legislation) were it not for the Eighth Amendment.

The inspiration for the Eighth Amendment campaign came from a fear that the 1973 US Supreme Court decision in *Roe -v- Wade* would be emulated by the Irish Supreme Court who would find a way of liberalising the law so as to achieve something similar to the English 1967 statute. This always seemed an unlikely possibility, given the Irish Supreme Court's approach to such matters. Nonetheless, the referendum was staged and two thirds of those voting (albeit under one half of the total electorate) voted for the form of words quoted above. The Irish Catholic bishops emphasised that each citizen should decide according to their own informed conscience, as with matters concerning contraception and divorce law. Some clergy, however, gave more enthusiastic support for the Eighth Amendment and nobody was in any doubt about the Church's general enthusiasm for this Amendment, though some clergy were sceptical.

SHAPING AN ABORTION LAW NOW

My own view is that any comprehensive abortion law in any jurisdiction would have to address four questions.

1. Who should decide?
2. On what grounds?
3. On the basis of what information?
4. Up to what time limit?

The debate in England, and to some extent the USA, has been locked into discussion of only the fourth point which is often a cover for one or more of the others. For example, the Oxford student abortion case *C. -v- S.* (1987) was ostensibly about the answer to question 4 but some would say that the father felt he should be one of the answers to question 1 and that the mother's grounds in answer to question 2 were inadequate. The Irish abortion debate has largely left question 4 to one side and focused on question 2 together with question 3 (at least in relation to abortions elsewhere and now, presumably to those abortions which are legal within the Republic – counsel for the government, for instance, conceded before the European Court of Human Rights that information would have to be allowed insofar as it related to those abortions which are lawful within Ireland under the Supreme Court's interpretation of the Eighth Amendment).

The emphasis on questions other than the time limit seems to me to be beneficial. On question 2, for example, there obviously are many people who believe that all grounds are acceptable and many who believe that no ground is acceptable but there are many more, in my opinion, who believe that even if all grounds are unacceptable, some are more unacceptable than others.

INFORMED CONSENT

On the third question, I find it astonishing that the enormous literature on informed consent has ignored the vital issue of what a woman would need to know before she could truly be said to have given informed consent to an abortion, while exhaustively analysing what patients should be told about virtually every other operation. Those who are pro-choice ought surely to be pro- an informed choice. Yet that lobby's opposition to the Pennsylvania law now before the U.S. Supreme Court suggests a lack of commitment to fully informed consent. Pennsylvania has legislated to require women contemplating an abortion to be told various details about the risks of the operation and the alternatives to it. Although the pro-choice lobby seems to see this as simply an example of piling up barriers to the quick availability of abortion, another way of looking at the statute is to say that it has called the bluff of those who designate themselves as pro-choice.

On the other side of this debate, it also seems to me that those who are pro-life ought to believe more in the power of their arguments. There would be less need for stricker laws of all sides could be sure that those contemplating an abortion were fully appraised of the pros and cons of such a decision.

The current challenge before the U.S. Supreme Court is part of a process of retreat from *Roe -v- Wade*. The disturbing intellectual legacy of that case has been to focus worldwide discussion on two aspect of abortion which, it seems to me, should not be at the centre of our arguments.

It is a relief, therefore, to see the Irish Supreme Court ignore the double mirage of *Roe -v- Wade*. There is no talk of the right to privacy and no suggestion (obviously, given the Eighth Amendment) that the unborn child is anything but a human being.

ABORTION LAW: THE TRAGIC CHOICES

There was a time (some would say twenty years) during which those agreeing with the result in *Roe -v- Wade* clung onto these elements of its strained reasoning. A better argument seems to be to accept that the foetus is a human being but to question what that means and to locate rights-based arguments in the non-discrimination rather than the privacy camp. Indeed, the internal contradictions of the privacy categorisation have helped to start the process of unravelling *Roe -v- Wade* as the claim that such a 'private' right should be publicly funded is examined.

RESPECTING WOMEN'S DIGNITY

Most commentary on *AG -v- X* (including this) commits the sin of legal fetishism, an undue obsession with the law. What matters is really the culture of society including its respect for the dignity of women and girls (the best way to stop fourteen-year-old girls seeking abortions is to stop fourteen-year-olds being raped), the availability of advice, the provision of practical help for those who prefer to continue with the pregnancy, etc. Ireland seems to believe itself to be a more moral country than many continental legal systems which allow abortion in almost unlimited circumstances, at least at the early stages of pregnancy. Yet if we acknowledge that some 5,000 Irish women seek abortions in England each year, then the pro-rata abortion rate from Ireland is probably higher than in the most 'lax' continental jurisdictions.

The law's role in the Irish abortion saga seems to be to provide a focus for public debate. Irish newspapers were reporting, for instance, that eight women from Ireland sought abortions in London clinics on any particular day during the currency of this case. This one girl's plight provided the opportunity for a nation to re-examine its attitudes to a tragic human problem. For all the words written on the matter, incidentally, the most poignant contribution came from the cartoonist Martyn Turner, in a sketch for the *Irish Times* of a girl clutching a teddy bear imposed on a map of the Republic of Ireland in which the land and sea borders are protected by barbed wire and the caption suggests that Ireland (after the High Court ruling) had introduced internment for fourteen-year old rape victims.

DEMOCRATIC FORCES

A last constitutional comment on this saga is to pick up a point about the way in which we resolve such problems in democracies. For many years I have been asking students to consider which method of law-making they would most prefer if they could guarantee that the result would be to their liking and I have urged them to consider this in the specific context of abortion, comparing the USA in which the Supreme Court made the running, England in which Parliament took the decisive steps, the Republic of Ireland where the people had their say in a referendum and Northern Ireland where, as ever, nobody got the chance to influence the law. This still seems to me a good question although *AG v X* is such a good illustration that it has spoiled the answer which I kept up my sleeve to the effect that these are not alternatives, that the politicians, courts and people all have a part to play in shaping abortion law.

MORAL IMPERATIVES

When the Irish Catholic bishops say in their statement criticising the Supreme Court that 'The protection of human rights, including the rights of the unborn, is a moral imperative for every society', sceptics will note that the Catholic Church, after shunning talk of rights for decades, has just adopted it when the rest of the world is beginning to appreciate its limitations.

The bishops are surely right to speak of a moral imperative to face social problems. But the law should not be the prime target – I repeat the point that the way to stop fourteen-year-old rape victims from seeking abortions is to stop them being raped. This is not something a law alone can achieve. It is a matter of social attitudes, of power, respect, morality, education. A truly pro-life Ireland would not need laws to restrain abortion, nor to restrict access to information, nor to intern travellers, since the conditions which give rise to abortion would have been addressed. As Grant Gilmore wrote, 'In Heaven there will be no law ... in Hell there will be nothing but law'.

DEFENDING MINORITIES

This side of Utopia, however, there obviously will be law regulating abortion. A long way from Utopia, Britain has abortion laws which, while at the opposite end of the spectrum of permissiveness, share a characteristic with the Irish position. Both Ireland and Britain ignore the underlying problems which lead to abortions. The British archbishops, however, have adopted an approach which merits examination on this side of the Irish Sea. First, they distinguish law and morality. Second, they locate their contribution to the public debate within a general concern for minorities. Third, they offer practical help while respecting autonomy in a dignified way.

As to the first, in their 1980 statement on the matter, the Catholic archbishops of Britain accepted 'a situation in which the requirements of the criminal law might reasonably be less demanding than those of a truly moral conscience'. Their example was where the mother's life could not be saved without an abortion:

> In such a situation, the law of God, which is also the rule of reason, makes exceptionally high demands. In reaffirming that law we are not asserting that the law of the land should treat as criminal the acts of someone who, in that situation, does not acknowledge or does not live up to those demands.

Second, the Catholic Church's teaching, however unpalatable to others, was put firmly in the context of defending minorities:

> Our stand against abortion is one aspect of our stand against all practices that degrade human rights ... The bishops have tried to defend the insulted, the despised, the disadvantaged ... The whole of Christian social teaching can be seen as an appeal to the conscience of the relatively well-off and powerful to give practical recognition to the humanity and rights of the poor and the weak.

Third, not only did the archbishops stress the need for positive help, but they also showed some sensitivity to the way in which such help should be offered:

> A girl or woman should always be given the practical help she may need to carry through her pregnancy. She should be given it unstintingly and without moral censure ... But it must always be given in a way that fully respects her freedom and responsibility.

Personal responsibility ought to be the primary target in all matters of morality. Of course, the law has a role to play but we should constantly be aware of its limitations and the danger of allowing it to become a false target, obscuring our failures to address more fundamental questions.

Vatican II Perspectives

LOUIS McREDMOND

The Second Vatican Council knew its mind on abortion. Its *Constitution on the Church in the Modern World* includes abortion in a list of 'infamies' and says that 'from the moment of its conception life must be guarded with the greatest care, while abortion and infanticide are unspeakable crimes'.

The present debate in Ireland, however, springs from a problem to which the Council did not advert. What should be done when there exists 'a real and substantial risk to the life, as distinct from the health, of the mother, which can be avoided only by the termination of her pregnancy'? The Supreme Court concluded that in such circumstances abortion was permitted.

In arriving at this decision the Court had *inter alia* to 'reconcile' and 'harmonise' the provisions of the Irish Constitution, in particular the guarantee of the unborn child's right to life together with the equal right of the mother provided in Article 40.3.3., and it had to consider questions of practicability raised by the wording of that Article.

The judges were manifestly painstaking and conscience-driven in discharging their duty. They made clear their commitment to the sanctity of human life and they gave carefully reasoned accounts of why and how they came to decide as they did – essentially because a circumstance faced them in which, as it appeared to them, the law could not be implemented in its entirety. This was not proclaiming an exception in the field of rights. It was identifying a factual situation in the field of medicine. They went on to say, for reasons given, what should be done.

This was not changing the law. It was indicating what the law meant in the factual situation for which they had to provide. It was also pointing out that the law had its limits, for the judges endorsed the dictum of a retired colleague that 'justice is not subordinate to the law.'

FOLLOWING A VOCATION

Such decisions, coming from such a source, would seem to merit that respect which the Vatican Council urged be granted to persons engaged in the discharge of functions appropriate to their vocation. Even when speaking specifically about the Catholic laity, the Council documents do so in terms which cannot be confessionally confined.

Thus, the *Constitution on the Church* points to the benefits which can accrue from the laity's 'competence in secular fields' and from an individual layman's 'knowledge, competence, or outstanding ability'. The *Laity Decree* tells the faithful to hold 'professional skill' in 'high esteem'. The *Constitution on the Church in the Modern World* stresses the need for citizens to 'observe the laws proper to each discipline' and it adds that, in these rapidly changing times, Church leadership must 'rely on those who live in the world, are versed in different institutions and specialties, and grasp their innermost significance'.

The Supreme Court is a body of persons distinguished for their knowledge, expertise and professional skill. Its judges observe the laws proper to their discipline, are versed more than anybody else in the institution to which they not only belong but which they collectively comprise, and are expected to elucidate the 'innermost significance' of their 'specialty'.

In the present case, the diligent and careful individual judgments recorded by the members of the Court, together with their use of yardsticks which happen to be conciliar as well as constitutional (they referred to prudence, justice and charity), called not for a moan of dismay or a howl of outrage but for a response of equal intellectual intensity and integrity. As of the time of writing, the judges' critics have yet to produce any response remotely as thoughtful.

SCIENTIFIC ADVANCE AND GOD'S WILL

The conciliar perspective also bears on the evidence which the majority of the judges found persuasive, namely, the opinion of 'a very experienced clinical psychologist' (as the Chief Justice described him) to the effect that the young mother in the case was likely to take her own life if the pregnancy continued. The reliability of such an opinion has been queried and the existence alleged of contrary opinions within the professions of psychology and psychiatry.

What matters in considering the significance of conciliar norms is not the accuracy of the expert opinion in a specific case but whether judges are entitled *in such cases* to give weight *to such evidence*. It is difficult to see why not, since the administration of justice requires judges daily to evaluate the evidence – open to contradiction – of physicians and surgeons. Why has science to halt at the physical? Psychology may have evolved as a branch of medicine later than surgery but it too can advance, make discoveries, acquire greater certitude.

The Council acknowledged this kind of growth in its *Modern World* document, which refers to 'profound and rapid changes ... triggered by the intelligence and creative energies of man'. The 'scientific spirit' is a sign of the times in which man progresses 'by relentlessly applying his talents' in accordance 'with God's will'. To *disparage* psychological evidence conflicts with the dynamism of history and scientific development lauded by Vatican II. It sits uneasily with the directive laid down for the Church by the Council to 'recognise and understand the world in which we live' and it queries the on-going clarification of man's nature seen by the Council as a welcome consequence of the way in which man perfects his world.

It does *not* follow that psychological evidence is *irrefutable*, only that it is *admissible*. Being admissible, it should not be discarded out of hand as it is by those who keep insisting, despite the psychologist, that they know better and that caring organisations like CURA had the answer to the young mother's misery. This pits an amateur against a professional opinion – the opinion, indeed, of the professional who had interviewed the young mother. It also minimises professional expertise and calls scientific progress into doubt. Neither attitude conforms to the mind of Vatican II, any more than the degradation of human dignity implicit in the approach which in effect says to troubled women: 'we will give you every help in coping with the awful predicament to which our intransigence condemns you'.

I am, of course, speaking of populist debating points, not of alternative competent and reasoned opinions. Nor do I presume to criticise the devoted work of CURA and others for women who seek the assistance they offer.

I repeat that the question relates to circumstances in which the rights of mother and child, in the judgment of those who must decide, *cannot* be implemented simultaneously and are therefore circumstances which cannot be coped with by that care which would in other cases protect both lives: a medical reality. That reality is not expunged by shouting it down with the offer of a solution fitted to the ideology of the people who offer it rather than designed to mitigate the plight of the victim.

OPENING THE FLOODGATES?

Then there is the warning against opening the floodgates, the theory that any relaxation in the laws will result in ever wider permissiveness, as allegedly happened in other countries. This all-purpose argument has been called into service against changing the law on contraception and divorce as well as abortion. It ignores the fact that in some countries (possibly most) society adopted permissive standards *before* these were acknowledged at law; in such cases permissiveness cannot be laid at the door of legislative laxity.

Indeed if, as has been claimed, proportionately more Irish pregnancies end in abortion (courtesy of English clinics) than Dutch pregnancies, it has to be seriously asked whether law is at all as central to moral behaviour as we are led to believe.

Be that as it may, the floodgates argument relies on the concept of the common good. This is invoked to prevent the concession of even legitimate demands lest a collapse of the social fabric should follow. People who think in these terms have no need to study the careful reasoning by which the judges worked their way towards a resolution of the abortion case. Fear of the floodgates eliminates the relevance of facts.

THE JUST REQUIREMENTS OF THE COMMON GOOD

The Vatican Council gives little encouragement to the use of the common good as underpinning for laws of draconian rigidity. The *Declaration on Religious Freedom* refers to aspects of the common good more than once, but always in qualified terms: it speaks of 'the *just requirements* of public order' and it links together as moral imperatives 'respect *both* for the rights of others ... *and* for the common welfare' [my italics]. In short, the common good cannot of itself be an absolute determinant. It must be strictly confined to what is necessary after every care has been taken to ensure that it is not being made into an excuse for unwarranted oppression.

Every care has hardly been taken when the solution to a dilemma, proposed for reasons given upon authority meriting respect, is met by blanket denunciation – not because the social order *will* collapse but because it is *feared* that the social order *might* collapse. A mere hypothesis, unsustained by scientific analysis or unanimous consensus, should surely never be allowed to overrule decisions meticulously arrived at by persons charged with the protection of public order at the highest level. Thomas Jefferson put it well long ago wqhen he said that 'to restrain the profession or propagation of principles on supposition of their ill tendency is a dangerous fallacy' since the 'judge of that tendency will make his opinions the rule of judgement', and he went on:

> It is time enough for the rightful purposes of civil government to interfere when principles break out in overt acts against peace and good order.

Nor is oppression much guarded against by whistling up the common good as a catch-all *non possumus* whenever it is suggested that moral issues in the public domain require serious examination in the light of contemporary realities and the Church's ever-deepening comprehension of its own doctrines.

As an aside, I may be permitted to recall that when Religious Freedom was under debate at the Vatican Council in September, 1965, the fear that the common good might be invoked to justify oppressive action was felt to be a real hazard. I well remember Fr Courtney Murray, S.J., the principal author of the *Declaration*, insisting the references to 'public order' would have to be limited to 'public order based on justice' – which in fact was done before the text was finalised, as can be seen from one of the quotations above.

FAMILY RIGHTS

Finally, two comments, related to one another. The Vatican Council in its *Laity Decree* described the family as 'the first and vital cell of society'. The Irish Constitution concurs, asserting in concepts taken from the encyclical *Divini Illius Magistri* that the family possesses 'inalienable and imprescriptible rights, antecedent and superior to all positive law'.

The Supreme Court some years ago indicated that among the rights given this elevated status is the family's authority to make decisions in its own regard. It will be recalled that in the recent case the family had consulted together and decided on abortion as the best way to cope with its agony. Those who argue that the judges, by meeting the family's wishes, offended against the intention of Article 40.3.3. have to say where they stand touching the rights of the family and how an item of positive law can be pleaded against the family's regulation of its own affairs. Yet again let me stress that the case was not about general principles (the equal rights of child and mother) but about a situation in which these principles could not be fully applied.

The second comment follows from the first. The family's decision would seem to have been very conscientiously taken. If the judges had refused to endorse it, it might well have been argued that the State through its judicial arm was coercing citizens in such a manner that they were restrained from acting in accordance with their conscientious beliefs. The Vatican Council, in the *Declaration on Religious Freedom,* denounces precisely such coercion and says that religious freedom, which guarantees the right not to be coreced in that manner, should be 'sanctioned by constitutional law' – the only specific requirement, so far as I know, ever made by the universal Church regarding the content of constitutional law.

Yes, the common good could be pleaded against the argument. But could it be pleaded in a situation where the question had been what to do when otherwise relevant principles could not be implemented? And in which decisions were manifestly arrived at under the guidance of conscience? I wonder ...

HERE I STAND ...

Lest what I have had to say in this article be misunderstood, let me end by briefly stating my personal position on abortion. I am against it. I reject the feminist 'right to choose' and I do not want 'exceptions' to be written into law if the mother's right to life can otherwise be protected. I believe it can be protected by practical recognition on the part of the law enforcement agencies (aided by their professional medical advisers) that cases arise in which the law *cannot* be implemented, that is, where the life of the child and the life of the mother *cannot* be given simultaneous protection.

I believe it to be inappropriate and unworkable to use the Constitution to make provision in these matters: a Constitution should set out broad principles (the right to life), not the application of these principles (whose life, in what circumstances). I would be happy if Article 40.3.3., which has worked so much mischief, could be rescinded in its entirety and Section 58 of the Offences against the Person Act left as the regulatory instrument which it used to be.

Simplistic? Perhaps. Impossible? I can think of half-a-dozen reasons, practical and legal, why what I believe desireable may now be unattainable. I would still like to see a solution pursued which would approximate as closely as possible to what I suggest rather than hand hostages to fortune by adding *more* words to the Constitution, needing *more* interpretation in the future. It is disingenuous to pretend that a constitutional clause can be drafted which will be immune to interpretation and provide an instant answer to every problem that will arise down the years out of the variety of human experience.

If you have difficulty in reconciling this account of where I stand with what went before, either you have not been reading my article with as much care as I employed in writing it, or else I lost touch with clarity in the pursuit of precision. Probably the latter. In which case, apologies.

What Is Christian Teaching on Abortion?

DAVID SMITH, M.S.C.

Christianity from its earliest days condemned abortion. It was regarded as sinful right from the moment of conception, although the gravity of the sin and the severity of the penalty varied, depending on whether the fetus[1] was 'unformed' or 'formed'. This tradition, which viewed abortion as always wrong, was carried over by the Reformers in the sixteenth and seventeenth centuries. At that stage in history it was accepted as part of the common Christian tradition.[2] Only in the seventeenth century did the theory of progressive ensoulment come to be questioned. Today the divergence between the Christian Churches on the gravity of abortion is centred around the status attributed to the fetus. Obviously a diversity of belief with regards to this crucial question will affect the ethics and practice of abortion.

Church Documents

THE ROMAN CATHOLIC CHURCH

The Catholic Church has never officially taught when the individual human being, endowed with a rational soul, begins in the mother's womb.[3] However, from the earliest times the Church taught the immorality of abortion at any stage after conception. She likewise condemned homicide and sanctioned canonical penalties for it. This led to the question of whether every abortion was also homicide or only if performed after a certain stage in pregnancy. In attempting to resolve this question the Church openly

---

1. Note on terminology: traditionally for the first two weeks the fertilized ovum is referred to as the *zygote* or *pre-embryo*. For the next five to six weeks, during the period of organogenesis, it is termed an *embryo*. From the eighth week onwards, it is referred to as a *fetus*. For clarity in this paper only the terms *fetus* and *embryo* will be applied.
2. Kevin Kelly, *Life and Love: Towards a Christian Dialogue on Bioethical Questions* (London: Collins, 1987), pp. 48. Hereafter this work will be referred to as Kelly.
3. Norman Ford, *When Did I Begin?* (Cambridge: Cambridge University Press, 1991), p. 57.

admits it was influenced by the commonly accepted view on the moment of ensoulment.

It is true that in the Middle Ages, when the opinion was generally held that the spiritual soul was not present until after the first few weeks, a distinction was made in the evaluation of the sin and the gravity of the penal sanctions. In resolving cases, approved authors were more lenient with regard to that early stage than with regard to later stages. But it was never denied at that time that procured abortion, even during the first few days, was objectively a grave sin. This condemnation was in fact unanimous.[4]

In other words the Catholic Church once assumed that the fetus did not become a human being until several weeks after conception. John Noonan maintains this remained the practice until 1869 when Pope Pius IX in the constitution *Apostolicae Sedis* dropped the reference to the 'ensouled fetus' in the excommunication for abortion so that the excommunication now seemed to include the abortion of any embryo.[5]

The Second Vatican Council was quite explicit in what it had to say about the value of life from the beginning:

> Life must be safeguarded with the utmost care from the moment of conception; abortion and infanticide are abominable crimes. (*Gaudium et Spes*,. 51).

The reason given for the careful wording of this statement was to avoid 'the difficult question of the moment at which the soul is infused.'[6] This teaching, which simply echoes the teaching of successive popes in recent years, is taken up and explained in much greater detail by the Congregation for the Doctrine of the Faith in its *Declaration on Procured Abortion*. Although appealing to scripture and tradition the document also demonstrates that its arguments make sense in the light of human reason. It argues:

> 12. ... In reality, respect for human life is called for from the time that the process of generation begins. From the time that

4. *Declaration on Procured Abortion*, issued by the Congregation for the Doctrine of the Faith, 18 November 1974, in *Vatican Council II: More Post-Conciliar Documents*, ed A. Flannery (Dublin: Dominican Publications, 1982), p. 443. Hereafter this work will be referred to as Flannery.

5. John Noonan, 'An Almost Absolute Value in History,' in *The Morality of Abortion: Legal and Historical Perspectives*, edited by John Noonan (London: Harvard University Press, 1977), p. 39.

6. Bernard Häring, in Vorgrimler (ed), *Commentary Documents of Vatican II*, Vol V, p. 243.

the ovum is fertilized, a life is begun which is neither that of the father nor of the mother; it is rather the life of a new human being with his own growth. It would never be made human if it were not human already.
13. This has always been clear, and discussions about the moment of animation have no bearing on it. Modern genetic science offers clear confirmation. It has demonstrated that from the first instant there is established the programme of what this living being will be: a man, this individual man with his characteristic aspects already well determined. Right from fertilization the adventure of a human life begins, and each of its capacities requires time – a rather lengthy time – to find its place and to be in a position to act. The least that can be said is that present science, in its most evolved state, does not give any substantial support to those who defend abortion. Moreover, it is not up to biological sciences to make a definitive judgment on questions which are properly philosophical and moral, such as the moment when a human person is constituted or the legitimacy of abortion. From a moral point of view this is certain: even if a doubt existed concerning whether the fruit of conception is already a human person, it is objectively a grave sin to dare to risk murder. 'The one who will be a man is already one' (Flannery, pp. 445-446).

Although not formally teaching that there is full human life present from the moment of fertilization, the document, owing to the 'risk of murder', rules out all abortions regardless of the stage of fetal development. This is stated more forcefully in the Apostolic See's *Chapter of the Rights of the Family* (23 October 1983):

> Human life must be respected and protected absolutely from the moment of conception.(Art. 4)

The stance of the Vatican is reiterated by various national episcopal conferences. The 1975 pastoral letter of the Irish hierarchy, *Human Life Is Sacred*, fully defended the Church's position. The 'abhorrent evil of abortion' was again pointed out in their 1985 pastoral, *Love Is for Life*. Commenting on the decision of the Irish Supreme Court in the recent case of a fourteen year-old rape victim the Irish bishops declared that abortion 'is the direct taking of innocent life and no motive can justify it. No court judgement, no act of legislation can make it morally right'

Owing to speculation regarding the status of the embryo raised by the increasing practice of *in vitro* fertilization and experimentation the Congregation for the Doctrine of the Faith felt it necessary to re-state the Catholic teaching in its *Instruction on Respect for Human Life in Its Origin and on the Dignity of Procreation.* Drawing substantially on the 1974 document its arguments can be summarised in four stages

1. As the life of the fertilised ovum is neither that of he father nor that of the mother, it is a *new* life.
2. This new life is a *human* life, for it could not be made human if it were not human already.
3. This new human life is the life of an *individual,* for *identity* is established from the first instant.
4. This *new human individual,* which comes into existence at the moment of conception, must surely be a person.[7]

Following a strategy of safety, the Roman Catholic Church, once again, reiterates its teaching that any risk of directly killing a full human being must be avoided. It, therefore, regards its absolute prohibition on direct abortion as definitive and unchangeable.

THE CHURCH OF ENGLAND

A considerable body in the Church of England has tended to pursue a developmental approach to the point of individuation when assessing the status of the fetus. This is aptly demonstrated in the recent publication of the Board for Social Responsibility, *Personal Origin*, which argues that consciousness must be seen as the distinctive feature of a human person. This is not a demand for the actual exercise of consciousness, but for the minimum conditions required for judging when there exists 'a subject capable in principle and in normal cases of exercising some rational and moral capacities.'[8] The implications of this understanding are found in the 1965 publication, *Abortion: An Ethical Discussion,* which remains the major Church of England statement dealing specifically with abortion.

While pointing out that the fetus has a moral significance inso-

7. Michael Coughlan, *The Vatican, the Law and the Human Embryo* (London: Macmillan, 1990), p. 65.
8. The Report of a Working Party on Human Fertilization and Embryology of the Board for Social Responsibility, *Personal Origins* (London: CIO Publishing, 1985), No. 89.

far as it is potentially a human life, it argues that the problem of abortion is precisely the problem of weighing the claims of the mother against the fetus and *vice versa*, when they conflict. It also draws attention to the fact that any discussion concerning abortion must not be seen in isolation, but in the context of the family group of which the mother and fetus are a part. The Statement therefore concludes that

> in certain circumstances abortion can be justified. This would be when, at the request of the mother and after the kind of consultation which we have envisaged in this report, it could be reasonably established that there was a threat to the mother's life or well-being, and hence inescapably to her health, if she were obliged to carry the child to term and give it birth. And our view is that, in reaching this conclusion, her life and well-being must be seen as integrally connected with the life and well-being of her family.... In our view such a consultative procedure could cover those cases where justification for abortion would rest upon there being an assessable risk of a defective or deformed child, as well as cases of incest or rape; though the ground of the decision would be the prognosis concerning the mother as affected by the pregnancy; not the possibility of deformity itself, not simply the fact (if established) of the act of incest or rape.[9]

The General Synod of 1983, while expressing concern for the increase in abortions in the United Kingdom, continued to recognise that 'in situations where the continuance of a pregnancy threatens the life of the mother a termination of pregnancy may be justified' (Kelly, p. 57). It also requested that society provide adequate and safe provisions to facilitate such situations.

THE METHODIST CHURCH

The Methodist Conference adopted a formal statement on abortion in 1976. The following year the Division of Social Responsibility of the Methodist Church produced a report giving the background to this statement and providing a commentary on it. It points out that all human life, because of its eternal, physical and material dimensions, should be reverenced. But the human being

---

9. Statement of the Churchof England Board for Social Responsibility, *Abortion: An Ethical Discussion* (London: CIO Publishing, 1965), pp. 61-62.

is created for relationships with the divinity and fellow human beings. However, in the case of the fetus, although it possesses a degree of individual identity it lacks independence and the ability to respond to relationships. Using this argumentation as background it states that when considering the matter of abortion 'the Christian asks what person, or beings who are properly to be treated wholly or in part as persons, are involved and how they will be affected by a decision to permit or forbid abortion.'[10] In its analysis it highlights two views: the inviolable right to life of the fetus; and the interests of the mother and her right to decide whether or not to continue the pregnancy. It concludes:

> Both views make points of real value. On the one hand, the significance of human life must not be diminished; on the other hand, abortion is unique because of the total physical dependence of the fetus on the mother, to whose life, capacities or existing responsibilities the fetus may pose a threat of which she is acutely aware. It is necessary both to face this stark conflict of interests and to acknowledge that others are also involved – the father, the existing children of the family, the extended family, and society in general (No. 7).

Pointing out that the fetus never lacks human significance from the moment of conception and that this significance increases with time, the report suggests that 'no pregnancy should be aborted after the point when the aborted fetus would be viable.' (No. 9)

The Methodist position, therefore, insists on respect for the fetus but it maintains that this respect should be in keeping with the fetus's developing human status. Conflicting interests of the mother and fetus, within the context of family and society, are influential criteria for assessing the ethics of abortion.

THE BAPTIST UNION OF GREAT BRITAIN AND IRELAND

The Baptist Union of Great Britain and Ireland, in their submission to the Warnock Committee, posed the question: 'When can human personality, as distinct from life only, be said to begin?' (Kelly, p. 63) In evaluating four possible moments – fertili-

---

10. John Atkinson (ed), *Abortion Reconsidered: The Methodist Statement and its Background* (London: Methodist Publishing House, 1977), No. 3. The following two quotations are from the same source.

zation; implantation; 'quickening'; and birth – it dismissed the latter two and concentrated on fertilization and implantation. It argued:

> After fertilization, the embryo has the potential to develop into a human being, but until implantation this potential cannot be realised. Life depends on a positive interaction with the environment for its sustenance and until implantation there is no such interaction.... Until a fetus is viable outside the womb it can only be a potential human personality, but it nevertheless deserves respect on precisely that account. Thus the question as to when personality begins cannot be answered absolutely, since man is a psychosomatic unity. But there is clearly an increasing weight of claim to respect as a 'potential personality', as the embryo increases in that potential....With increasing growth of an embryo the greater would need to be the weight of argument for altering or terminating that potential personality. (Kelly, p. 64)

The Baptist Union, a loose and voluntary alliance, advocates a similar approach to that of the Methodists.

Theological Approaches

SOME ROMAN CATHOLIC THEOLOGIANS

Many Catholic theologians believe that since theology is confronted with a clear and unchangeable doctrine of the ordinary Magisterium, there remains only the necessity of explaining clearly the reasons behind the doctrine and discussing whether some complicated cases might be considered as 'indirect abortion'. This, according to the principle of 'double effect', can be justified when the directly intended action is not abortion but a licit medical intervention that has the character of a remedy for the mother in a life threatening situation. In these instances the physician is allowed to perform all medically accepted operations even if these medical procedures entail a probable or even certain danger to the life of the fetus as an undesired and indirect consequence.

The application of the 'double effect' principles is not easily discernable in all life-threatening situations. In these cases Catholic moral theologians like Bernard Häring, Franz Boeckle and others argue that it is not a matter of preferring either the life of the mother to the child, or the child to the mother, but a choice between the life that can be saved and the life that cannot. In these instances the sole choice is to let both die or save the life of the mother. In such an intervention, the child is already deprived of any chance to be kept alive, and its conscious life is shortened by only a brief period.[11]

In a further development of this argumentation Haring considers situations in which the continuation of pregnancy, although not life threatening, would cause 'grave damage' to the mother. He maintains:

> I consider probable the opinion of those who justify the removal of a fetus that surely cannot survive, when the action is taken in order to prevent grave damage to the mother. For instance, an anencephalic fetus not only cannot develop into a conscious human life but cannot even survive. To remove it in order to spare great damage to the mother is truly therapeutic while no injustice is done to the life of this fetus already doomed to death (*Free and Faithful in Christ*,Vol. 3, p. 34).

Although he does not elaborate on the meaning of 'grave damage' he still regards this type of intervention as 'indirect abortion'.

In his application of these principles to daily life Häring draws a distinction between moral theology and pastoral counselling.[12] Moral theology, he states, operates on a level 'where questions are raised about general rules or considerations that would justify a particular moral judgement.' Pastoral prudence, however, looks to the art of the possible. Thus, when considering rape it is morally permissible to cleanse away the sperm, which is considered to be an extension of the initial act of aggression. Abortion, is not allowed if conception has already taken place. It cannot be concluded that the fetus, which would not have been formed except for the presence of the 'aggressive' sperm, is itself an 'aggressor'.[13]

Nevertheless, it must be recognised that although the fetus is innocent, the girl likewise is innocent. Her revulsive feelings that

---

11. Bernard Häring, *Free and Faithful in Christ*,Vol. 3 (Middlegreen, Slough, St Paul Publications, 1981), p. 33.
12. Bernard Häring, *Medical Ethics* (Middlegreen,Slough: St Paul Publications, 1982), p. 112 ff.
13. Bernard Häring, *Shalom: Peace. The Sacrament of Reconciliation* (New York: Farrar,Strauss and Giroux), 1968), p. 181.

this is not 'her' child which she is in justice required to bear are understandable. The Catholic counsellor should try to motivate her to consider the child with love because of its subjective innocence, and to bring it to term. If, owing to the psychological effects of her traumatic experience, she is utterly unable to accept this counsel, it is possible that she should be left in 'invincible ignorance'. 'Invincible ignorance', a traditional term in catholic theology refers to the existential wholeness of the person, the over-all inability to cope with a certain moral imperative. This inability can exist not only with regard to the highest ideals of the gospel, but also with regard to the particular prohibited norm. On this basis Haring concludes that the counsellor should not pursue the question once it had become evident that the woman could not bear the burden of pregnancy, not bear the burden of a clear appeal not to abort.[214]

Stanley Hauerwas, of Notre Dame University, approaches the morality of abortion from a different viewpoint. He begins by examining three questions relating to abortion: When does life begin? When may life be taken legitimately? What does the agent understand to be happening? Having answered the first two in classical terms he turns to the third question. He contends that there is more in an agent's deliberation and decision that are morally important than in the spectator's judgement. This 'more' is the agent's perspective. To illustrate how this perspective works he takes a situation presented by the Protestant theologian, James Gustafson – a very tragic instance of pregnancy resulting from multiple rape in a situation of poverty, illness, and lack of employment. Gustafson argues that because the pregnancy resulted from a sex crime and the social and emotional conditions for the well-being of the mother and child are not advantageous, the abortion would be morally justified.

Hauerwas defends Gustafson's approach, not on the basis that abortion is a good thing, but rather because 'abortion morally is justified under an ethical perspective that tries to pull as much good as possible from the situation.' It might be different if societal conditions and the woman's biography favoured and supported carrying the pregnancy to term. Hauerwas claims that

---

14. Bernard Häring, ' A Theological Evaluation', in John Noonan (ed.), *The Morality of Abortion: Legal and Historical Perspectives* (London: Harvard University Press, 1977), pp. 140-143.

moral choices do not occur an ideal conditions where right and wrong are apparent, but rather the right must be wrenched from less than ideal alternatives.[15]

A PROTESTANT ETHICAL APPROACH

The practical implications of the Churches who follow the developmental approach are expanded by various theologians. Owing to the frequent reference to these arguments in any discussion on abortion it is worthwhile to examine at least two of them.

Three principles and three exceptions summarize James Gustafson's position.

1. Life is to be preserved rather than destroyed.
2. Those who cannot assert their own rights to life are especially to be protected.
3. There are exceptions to these rules.
  Possible exceptions are:
  a. 'medical indications' that make therapeutic abortion morally viable.
  b. the pregnancy has occurred as a result of sexual crime. (I would grant this as a viable possible exception in every instance ... if the woman herself was convinced that it was right. If the woman sees the exception as valid, she has a right to more than a potentially legal justification for her decision; as a person she has the right to understand why it is an exception in her dreadful plight.)
  c. the social and emotional conditions do not appear to be beneficial for the well-being of the mother and the child. (In particular circumstances, this may appear to be justification, but I would not resort to it until possibilities for financial, social, and spiritual help have been explored.)[16]

What is crucially important to Gustafson is compassion for the woman involved, and her ability to make a human decision grounded in freedom of choice. Nevertheless, seeing the tragedy of abortion, he, with an allusion to war, argues that as the morally conscientious soldier fighting in a particular war is convinced that

15. Richard McCormick, *Notes on Moral Theology: 1964 through 1980* (University Press of America, 1981), pp. 500-501.
16. James Gustafson, 'A Protestant Ethical Approach' in *The Morality of Abortion: Legal and Historical Perspectives*, edited by J. Noonan (London: Harvard University Press, 1977), p. 116.

life can and ought to be taken, 'justly' but also 'mournfully',[17] so the moralist can be convinced that the life of the defenceless fetus can be taken, less justly, but more mournfully.[18]

An ordained minister and consultant gynaecologist, R. F. Gardner, was instrumental in assisting to develop the Christian mind on the question of abortion in Britain. In his justification of abortion he argues that the fetus does not possess a soul, and therefore we are not considering the destruction of a human life destined for eternity. He suggests that it is when the child takes his or her first breath that the soul enters the body.[19] Three 'scientific pointers' are offered to support this thesis. First, the question of identical twins. At some point after conception, and sometimes even after implantation, the embryo divides into two. 'Unless', writes Gardner, 'we are to agree with the suggestion that the soul splits likewise we are driven to conclude that in some cases at least its infusion is not before the fourth week of intrauterine life.' Secondly, he draws attention to the phenomenon of fetal 'wastage' whereby 'anything up to half of all conceptions end in spontaneous miscarriages, usually very early on'. He considers it inconceivable that God should fill his heaven with these young lives, and concludes that it is evidence of the absence of 'spiritual status' on the part of the fetus. Thirdly, to suggest that embryos cultured in vitro and experimented upon and then disposed of possess a soul would be to trivialize the 'meaning of the soul.'

Having disposed of the 'spiritual status' of the fetus Gardner advances his own grounds for justifying abortion. His starting-point is Christian compassion. 'Real compassion', he suggests, 'involves taking into account medical and social factors.' His compassionate aim is not just to alleviate a woman's short term problem, but also to facilitate a better future life for her. However, he does point out, that for the Christian physician, it is not just a matter of responding to a distressing situation but trying to determine the will of God in that particular situation. His discernment process for arriving at a decision appears to be an examination of the physical, psychological, spiritual, social and economic factors which impact on the life of his patient.

17. Roland Bainton, *Christian Attitudes towards War and Peace* (New York: Abingdon Press, 1960), p. 98.
18. J. Gustafson, 'A Protestant Ethical Approach', p. 122.
19. R. F. Gardner, *Abortion: the Personal Dilemma* (London: Exeter, 1972), p. 126. The following three quotations are also from this work, pp. 123 and 131.

For these theologians, and those who agree with their ethics, the defence of abortion generally operates on the principle of denying to the fetus, at some stage or at all stages, the respect due to full human life outside the womb.[20]

UNITY IN DIVERSITY

As can be observed from this brief survey of certain Christian Churches all agree that the human embryo has 'value' and must be respected. The disagreement concerns what precisely is the 'value' of the human embryo. One view, represented explicitly by the Roman Catholic Church, states that it has exactly the same value as any other human being. Another view, represented by a strong body of opinion in the Church of England, asserts that its value, prior to individuation (consciousness), is less than that of a human being in the proper sense of the word. A third view, represented by the Methodist Conference, would argue that its value depends on its stage of development: thus a progressively increasing value. The Baptist Union seems to favour a similar position, as does the Church in Wales and the Free Churches. (Kelly, p. 65)

The implications of these approaches for abortion are quite clear. When the value given to the embryo is exactly the same as that given to any other human being, then the good of the embryo cannot be directly sacrificed for the good of any other human beings involved. This view, therefore rules out every act of direct abortion. When full human value is given to the embryo only after the point of definitive individuation has been reached, then prior to that moment the good of the embryo takes second place when it is in conflict with full human beings. If the human embryo is considered to have less-than-fully-human but progressively increasing value up to the time of birth, then respect for full human dignity would justify abortion right through the whole of pregnancy. According to this view, it would be a violation of human dignity to subordinate the good of a human being to that of a being, despite its intrinsic value, which is not fully human. The reasons for abortion, however, would need to increase in gravity in proportion to the lateness of the pregnancy. (Kelly, pp. 75-76)

---

20. Nigel Cameron and Pamela Sims, 'Defending Abortion', *Ethics and Medicine* 2:3 (1986), p. 38.

FREEDOM AND THE LAW

With these diverse views on the morality of abortion, numerous states have legislated for abortion where the fetus is perceived to be a direct threat to the life of the mother, or where the fetus is seen to endanger the 'health' of the mother. 'Health in this sense can have a very broad interpretation depending on how it is defined in various legal traditions. Catholics, Häring advises, although they might not find the reasons concerning a broad definition of health convincing, should not oppose the legislation of a pluralistic state that freedom in those cases to the physicians and the mothers to decide according to their conscience.[21]

---

21. Bernard Häring, *Free and Faithful in Christ*, Vol. 3, p. 34.

Laylines

SEÁN MAC RÉAMOINN

The caption *Laylines* is particularly apt this month. For I write not only as one who is neither cleric nor theologian, but also without legal, medical, philosophical or sociological expertise. Nor can I claim to be one of those most closely affected by abortion law or practice. Still, as a citizen, as a husband and father, and as a Christian, I *am* affected. It's not just a matter of *nihil humanum a me alienum*. Abortion is not only a 'personal' or a 'private' issue: like birth and death it touches society, that is to say all of us, directly or indirectly. Which is, I suppose, why it can and does become a matter of law.

When I say society, I am thinking especially of *our* society, here in Ireland. And I'm afraid that, for the purposes of the present debate, this means the Republic. Not that we can, even if we wished to, ignore the curious situation in the North, which is in some ways closer to our own than to that in Britain. Also our Churches have still an 'All-Ireland' base, and the historic Archdiocese of Armagh straddles the political border.

But our immediate situation, arising from the Supreme Court decision on the appeal against a High Court injunction in the case of *AG -v- X.*, is a matter for the citizens of the Republic. And my personal concern is to try to see what we, the Roman Catholic people who form the great majority of these citizens, should seek or demand or support by way of legislation, so that the law of this Republic may reflect the will of the people as a whole.

Not just the Catholic will, though this must naturally, and properly, count for a great deal. David Smith's article outlines the common Christian teaching on abortion, as well as certain differences within the Churches pointing to a diversity of praxis. Patrick Hannon and Louis McRedmond consider how the Catholic legislator and the Catholic voter may take account of these and other divergences in a pluralist society, in the light of certain insights and pronouncements of the Second Vatican Council, based (in Professor Hannon's words) 'on the dignity of the person and on the nature of the search for truth'.

Before proceeding further, we must heed Simon Lee's warning against making law 'a false target for morality' at the expense of personal responsibility in an actual social context. The figure of 5,000 Irish women seeking abortions in England each year, reflects very oddly on our 'more moral than thou' attitude to other jurisdictions which facilitate abortions but whose 'turnover' is, he suggests, probably lower *pro-rata* than ours. I would only add a reminder that the real figure is almost certainly appreciably higher still, to include those who do not claim or admit an Irish domicile.

And what of those who quite simply cannot afford to travel? Are we sure that the 'back-street' operator is no longer with us? Indeed, one of the nastiest aspects of the situation here is the way it imposes on the poor and helpless a morality which those who can afford it may evade. Over these last weeks I have been haunted by the thought of Ann Lovett and her baby in a Longford field ...

When I speak of a morality being 'imposed', I do not of course suggest that the moral principle of the sacredness of human life is not freely accepted by nearly all of us. I mean rather that there is a way out for 'hard cases', though at a price which not all can pay. At a much deeper level indeed there is the kind of 'imposition' which is resented by those who proclaim *the woman's right to choose*. This phrase is, as I have suggested here on another occasion, patient of a legitimate moral interpretation, inasmuch as any moral act is authentic only if freely chosen. But here we have one of the many instances where morality and law can be at odds.

THE PEOPLE ARE SAYING ...

But before we consider what Irish law should say or do in response to a prevailing morality (with or without variations in detail) we must have a look at two other words. These are *mores* and *politics*. The political dimension is the easier (if not the simpler) as it makes us come to terms with the fact that, in a democracy, a government's efforts to govern, and an opposition's vocation to oppose, may often run counter to what is morally desirable. The 'art of the possible' may well involve strategies of compromise, of a rescheduling of priorities, even of a certain dilution of principle, which occasion a move away from what has become known as the 'high moral ground'. The move may be a temporary, tactical flit or a more permanent exodus: in either case, a return will depend largely on external pressure. This pressure may come from public opinion, but this is a notoriously unstable force.

Which brings me to the matter of *mores*, what visiting commentators on Irish life used to call our 'manners and customs'. Contemporary use of the word distinguishes it from 'morals' or 'ethics', but there is a certain overlap, sometimes of a serious nature. Thus, it is quite common nowadays for young people of both sexes to share a house or apartment for reasons of economic convenience. The accepted intimacies which this involves are a matter of *mores*, up to a certain point, when questions of sexual morality may arise. At a time of rapid cultural change it is easy to confuse the one with the other, and it is important that judgements based on this confusion are avoided.

But it must be recognised that shifts in a community's *mores* may have a lasting effect on the culture of that community, influencing social attitudes and public opinion. And this influence will by no means be confined to the generation who initiate change: it may quite rapidly occasion a break with the past, across the community as a whole. On the subject of abortion there has been such a break, in a comparatively short time, in the common discourse of Irish people, urban and rural. Even twenty years ago the word was used, if at all, only in discreet, even furtive, tones. And I would venture to suggest that the campaign preceding the 1983 referendum was a watershed. Fr Fergal O'Connor's words were surely prophetic:

> But whatever the answer about the moral character of the referendum, we should not let ourselves be confused about the real nature of abortion. In some ways it is far easier to present the case for it than against it. That is the story of its growth everywhere. For that reason we may well look back and see that it was very unwise to start this campaign at all. When all the words have flowed and the ink is dry, it is highly probable that more people will favour abortion than did before the debate, and that public opinion will have shifted somewhat towards accepting abortion as part of our medical services. The best 'reflectors' of public opinion are the young who absorb it unconsciously, and already many of them are ambivalent on the issue. (*Abortion and Law*, ed. A. Flannery, 1983, Dublin, Dominican Publications, p. 113)

This 'ambivalence', in discourse at least, is no longer confined to the young. But it does not necessarily mean that human life has become widely devalued in these recent years: indeed 'ambivalence' towards killing in the name of patriotism has, happily, shown a marked decrease, in the Republic at any rate. And here we may have a clue to the decline in horror where abortion is concerned. For, unfortunately, it seems to me that ending a pregnancy is commonly regarded as a question of *sexual* morality – a matter of the 'Sixth' rather than the 'Fifth' (if such categories mean anything still). For all the 'Pro-Life' emphasis on 'killing babies', there is wide current of public opinion which rejects this as so much rhetoric, and disgusting rhetoric at that. Abortion has become a sexual 'right' (or a sexual sin), along with divorce and contraception: it does not belong, as it should, with murder, manslaughter, death on the roads, assassination, capital punishment, the mass killings of war, or the mass deaths of plague and famine. Nor will quoting the figures of world-wide wholesale abortion produce a reaction anything like that which some of the Holocaust statistics continue (very properly) to evoke.

It may be argued that my list, beginning with murder and ending with famine, is ill-chosen and ill-assorted. While they all involve the taking of human life and so must be seen as evil, the degree of evil and the imputation of guilt are widely divergent – in some cases there's no guilt at all.

NECESSARY EVILS

In fact the assortment was deliberate on my part, in order to underline a point too often forgotten in our present debate. For the absolutist tone of the great bulk of anti-abortion propaganda is, I believe, self-defeating. To declare that life in the womb has an utterly inviolable right to survive must immediately provoke the question: why in the womb only? – since such an absolute right has never been sustained elsewhere. I don't have to give details of the circumstances in which Christian authority throughout the centuries has not only tolerated but at times actively encouraged the ending of human lives, often in the name of Christ himself. Cromwell and his officers were worthy successors to the torturers and executioners of the Inquisition. And there are many among us today – Christian, Jew, Muslim and humanist – who, while recognising that the taking of life, on the battlefield or in 'legal' execution, is an evil, would claim it to be a *necessary* evil ... Can this never be the case with life in the womb? And if not, why not? These are questions to which I have yet to hear a convincing answer.

Such attempts at an answer as have been offered usually rely on qualifying the idea (or fact) of human life with the word 'innocent'. It is a highly emotive word, not least in the present context. As commonly understood, it implies freedom from moral guilt: it is applied in a general sense to young children and sometimes to the mentally ill or handicapped, but specifically to those guiltless of a particular crime or misdemeanour. In both of these senses it clearly applies to the unborn (except perhaps in regard to Original Sin!)

But its moral relevance is far from clear. For, while the death of the 'innocent' is always to be deplored, few of us would now argue that the 'guilty' are fair game. No, if the word 'innocent' is of any importance in the context of the right to life, and I believe it is, we must see it in its original meaning of 'not harmful' (*in-nocens*). A psychotic who murders may be *free of guilt*, but, if there is a real danger of his doing it again, he cannot be regarded as 'not harmful': and, if immediately *nocent*, he may, perhaps must, in an emergency, be pre-emptively killed.

Now if one believes (as I do) that *all* human life is sacred and that to end it is evil, the killing of the psychotic is surely still evil, but *necessary,* or *the lesser of two.* To apply this principle to the unborn must be a matter of the greatest delicacy, but I have long argued that it is the best approach to the problem of 'exceptions' or 'hard cases'. Happily in the vast majority of instances the living foetus is indeed 'innocent' in the sense of *not harmful:* the tiny minority that are not, and may constitute a real threat to the mother, must be the only cases where the deliberate termination of a pregnancy may be morally justified. I would emphasise 'may be': the onus of proof that the evil is in fact necessary must rest on those who would propose termination.

This is the moral framework within which I would propose legislative development. That such development is an urgent requirement is, I think, generally agreed, but on its form and status, as well as its thrust, there is little or no consensus.

AFTER MAASTRICHT

I have no wish to go again over well-trodden ground in regard to our present constitutional/legislative dilemma, on either the national or European levels. As to the immediate future, I am personally in agreement with the Taoiseach's decision to hold a referendum on the Maastricht treaty as soon as possible, and to deal with the abortion issues afterwards, but without undue delay.

If I may deviate briefly, it is to be devoutly hoped that public debate on Maastricht will be confined to a discussion of the pros and cons of the Treaty. It would be tragic if irrelevancies, however important in themselves, were allowed so to darken counsel as to provoke a negative vote (or a widespread abstention) based on extrinsic considerations. In particular, persons of influence in the community, including Church leaders, should urge people to vote on the merits of the Treaty, not least because of the moral scare-mongering of some who should know better. Any suggestion that the issue is one of moral principle as against material gain is merely empty but dangerous rhetoric, and should be exposed as such. A firm statement by the Catholic bishops to this effect is surely called for.

But after Maastricht, whatever way the referendum goes, the government is left with the urgent business of legislation. The Supreme Court judgement cannot be ignored. Does it demand further constitutional change? Apart from my personal wish for the repeal of Article 40.3.3, which I realise is highly improbable, I cannot see any possible amendment as necessary or desirable. Enough has been said by others to encourage me in this view, so I will not labour it here.

Parliamentary legislation is another matter, and I am under no illusion that the process of drafting will be easy. Nor do I see any likely measure as either having an easy passage through the Oireachtas, or being assured of a majority vote in either house. The only aspect of the matter which would probably find acceptance on all sides is the principle of freedom to travel, though even there I can see possible difficulties in detail. Freedom of information is hardly likely to prove generally acceptable, but probably some compromise can be agreed.

But, in fact, these two points are, while important in themselves, only marginal to the central issue which the Supreme Court appears to have forced on our urgent consideration. I mean the possible legality of an abortion induced within the jurisdiction of the Republic. Unthinkable though this might have seemed up to a few months ago, now we must all think, and think hard, about it.

Such a move will of course be very widely resisted on moral

grounds. But I have to say that such 'moral' opposition must, in the actual Irish situation, involve a great deal of self-deception. The facts and figures of our current 'export' practice must surely insist that we ask the question: are the values of the Gospel, the sanctity of human life, and specifically the welfare of both mother and unborn child, best served by a policy which occasions this practice and apparently accepts it?

Or would a limited provision for 'lawful' abortion as a *necessary evil* in certain well defined circumstances be morally preferable? I am convinced that the question should at least be asked and seriously discussed. And I am also convinced that if it is not, it will present itself again and again in even less favourable circumstances.

DISTASTEFUL CHALLENGE

The kind of legislation I have indicated would of course need very careful consideration. But I don't think it beyond the wit of our legislators ... perhaps it should be preceded by a discussion document to encourage realistic and informed debate. And, since there would appear to be a general moral consensus on the nature of abortion, and a rejection of its acceptance as common practice, it would go a long way to meet the strongly-held convictions of certain Christian bodies, and of other morally concerned people, who cannot accept what they see as the 'strict' Catholic line. Nor should there be any valid Catholic objection – see the 'four rules' noted in the penultimate paragraph of Professor Hannon's article (p. 252).

I know that some of us are reluctant to accept the idea of a 'necessary evil' in moral argument. Personally, and I think I am not alone in this, I find it more cogent than the 'principle of double effect'. In fact either formula can be misused, and it would be very foolish indeed to base legislation on any loose application of either. But the basic idea of the necessary evil (or the lesser of two) is grounded in reality, and we all make it a rule-of-thumb in our daily doings. Naturally, in matters (literally) of life or death we are wise to use it very gingerly. But, properly understood and applied, it remains sound.

Up to now our legislators have not had to face what must be one of the most distasteful challenges in the whole business of politics. I cannot see the present 'export-only' situation continuing indefinitely. Inaction can only mean postponement, and, whatever chance there now exists of reasonable debate and sensible balanced legislation, polarisation and anger make future prospects look dim indeed.

Pointers to an adequate law are to be found in Professor Lee's article, and would repay study. I found his remarks on 'informed consent' particularly interesting, and suitable to our situation. He also has wise things to, say about the 'slippery slope' or 'floodgates' argument, which Ricca Edmundson also subjects to a measure of cool analysis. Unfortunately those who advocate this argument against change in any *status quo* are notoriously impervious to factual rebuttal. But it is at least possible to hope that careful legislation might lead, not to a campaign for 'abortion on demand' but, on the contrary, to a marked decline in the present 'export' figures and a very small number of abortions here.

I shouldn't have to add that new legislation, however well drafted, can only tackle one end of the problem. CURA and similar organisations will be needed more than ever, and sex education, in the fullest sense, continues to be an urgent priority. And it remains true that until the dignity of women and their place in society is given proper recognition, they will continue to be used as sex objects, with often disastrous consequences.

Indeed I have said little about the centrality of the woman in this whole discourse, apart from the question of her 'right to choose'. It is all too easy, when arguing the pros and cons of pregnancy and abortion, for men to forget this centrality, and to ignore the profound implications of law and morality on the most personal level of all. Hers, in a very real sense, must be the last word.

Documents

The major Vatican document, referred to by David Smith in 'What Is Christian Teaching on Abortion' is the DECLARATION ON PROCURED ABORTION (1974) by the Sacred Congregation for the Doctrine of the Faith, full text in Austin Flannery (ed.) *Vatican Council II: More Post-Conciliar Documents*, 1984, Dublin, Dominican Publications, pp. 441-453.

Yes to Life*

BISHOPS OF IRELAND

RESPECT FOR LIFE

1. Human life is sacred, even before it is born. Sexuality and sexual love are sacred, as the mysterious source of human life. These truths have been honoured by the great majority of men all through history, whatever their religion and whatever their culture.

2. Christians in particular have, until recently, been unanimous and undivided in their absolute respect for the unborn life and in their view of what reverence for sex, the source of life, implies. These values have begun to be questioned only in recent years. It is necessary for us all to examine these matters again in the light of the Gospel and in the light of Christian and human conscience.

3. It is our Christian faith which provides our deepest insight into the mystery of life and the surest guidance as to how life is to be respected. The Church has centuries of experience in dealing with men in all cultures and in all conditions. All this wise experience lies behind her judgments on human living. But her faith is much more than merely human insight: it is a sharing in the mind of Christ. St Paul says: 'We teach, not in the way in which philosophy is taught but in the way that the Spirit teaches us, showing how spiritual truths make spiritual sense ... we are those who have the mind of Christ' (1 Cor 2:13-16).

The teaching of the Church, guided by the Holy Spirit of Christ, gradually forms in us 'the same mind which was also in Christ Jesus' (Phil 2:5). We have, therefore, an obligation to form our beliefs and consciences in the full light of the teaching of the Church. This Pastoral Letter has been written in order to set out the teaching of the Church in the matter of human life and its origins in marriage.

* Extract from the pastoral letter, *Human Life Is Sacred*.

THE VALUE OF LIFE

4. The Christian principle of respect for human life at every stage of its existence is firm and clear. God alone is the Lord of life. Man is made in his image and likeness. We come from God. We go to God. We belong to God. In the Psalms we read: 'Know that he, the Lord, is God. He made us, we belong to him' (Ps 99:3). 'For it was you who created my being, knit me together in my mother's womb. I thank you for the wonder of my being' (Ps 138:13-14).

God's commandment, 'Thou shalt not kill', unconditionally forbids all taking of innocent human life from its beginnings in the womb until the end that God, not man, has set for it. One must have absolute respect for human life as coming from God's hands at the very first moment of conception and as remaining under God's care on earth until he takes it back to himself again in death.

5. Some will argue that not every life is of equal value. But in the eyes of God every life is of equal and of priceless value. We must see every life as having the value which it has for God. Christ speaks of the loving concern for each one of us which God has as our most dear Father: 'Can you not buy two sparrows for a penny? And yet not one falls to the ground without your Father knowing. Why, every hair on your head has been counted. So there is no need to be afraid; you are worth more than hundreds of sparrows' (Matt 10:29-31).

Each human being is called to live with God forever. Each human being is one of whom Christ thought so much that he died for him. Here is where each human being gets his value. Some people have answered the question, 'What is that man worth?', by stating the value of his assets or the amount of his annual earnings. The true answer is: 'That man is worth the life's blood of Christ'. There and only there is the true standard for judging the value of life.

6. Secular society has different priorities in its attitudes and laws. In many countries State law has come to allow abortion for a variety of reasons. The changes in the law which brought this about would no~ have been introduced unless public opinion had first been lulled by propaganda; but when changes of this kind in the law are introduced they change public opinion still further and much more rapidly in the same direction. Abortion is now discussed in many countries almost as if it raised no moral problem at all. People talk now instead as if the only problem were to find ways of making abortion still more widely available, faster and cheaper.

7. In this Letter, we are speaking primarily on the basis of our faith in Christ. We are speaking primarily to those who share that faith. But we confidently appeal also to the 'unwritten laws' of the Creator, which can be seen by human reason to be written in God's creation, and to be engraved in the heart of man, in his conscience and his sense of personal re-

sponsibility. During the whole of its history until very recently, and even before Christianity, the ethics of the medical profession found its cherished expression in the Hippocratic Oath. By the terms of this oath, already five hundred years before Christ, doctors solemnly swore: 'I shall never, no matter who may demand it, supply a homicidal drug ... I shall never supply any woman with an abortive pessary. By chastity and sanctity, I shall protect my life and my profession.'

A more modern form of this Oath, the Geneva Medical Oath, drawn up in 1948 by the World Health Organisation, says: 'I shall keep absolute respect for human life, from the moment of conception.'

We are therefore at one with the oldest and noblest traditions of the medical profession when we take our stand for the sacred character and the absolute rights of unborn life. We are also at one with the deepest convictions of the human conscience.

8. When the Church states her moral principles, however, she appeals ultimately to the truth and love which Christ brought into the world. She takes the divine Teacher as her model. She endeavours to speak clearly and without compromise; but she speaks with love for the human person, with respect for human intellect and for human freedom; and she speaks with the confidence that the inner force of the Christian message will, by God's grace, and because of its sheer truth and rightness, find an answering echo in the heart of man.

ABORTION IS KILLING THE INNOCENT

9. God's commandment, as we have seen, is that no human being may deliberately take away innocent human life. What life could be more innocent than that of the unborn child? Deliberate abortion is therefore always gravely sinful. The embryo or foetus possesses its fundamental right to life from the moment of conception. From that moment the foetus is already provided with all the genetic elements which will shape its future development as an adult human person. To use the language of genetics, the embryo, from the instant of the meeting of the mother and father cells, is already equipped with the entire 'programme' of its future physical characteristics, right down to the minutest detail (including its unique and identifying fingerprints), as well as of its basic mental capacity and personality traits. Everything that education and environment will later have to work on is already present in the embryo. Each single embryo, even though so small as to be invisible to the naked eye, is unique and unrepeatable. Strictly speaking, so far as in-built potential for future development is concerned, the newly-fertilised mother-cell has the same potential as the newly-born baby. A distinguished Professor of Midwifery has said: 'This is more than a potential human being; it is already a human being with potential, complete with every genetic detail, unique, individual and unrepeatable.'

From the day of conception to the day of birth, life in the womb is a continuing process of inter-locking events. To interrupt the process is to take innocent human life.

10. How could women and girls ever think of having an abortion performed if they realised the wonder and the beauty of the tiny being that is living and growing close to their heart? How can men be so heartlessly insensitive to the deepest feelings of women, so blind to the mysteries of parenthood, as to pressurise their partners into seeking abortions? Once their child is conceived, they are not about to become parents: they have become parents already. Any mother who has had the sorrow of a miscarriage knows that it was a baby that she lost.

11. The likeness of the parents is already stamped on the little being from the beginning. The human organs and features develop with astonishing rapidity. Before the first month is out, head and brain-cells, mouth and eyes are there. By the end of the fourth week, the beating of the heart has been detected. In the sixth or seventh week, the foetus will respond to a touch. Many abortions take place at twelve weeks. By then the baby has well developed features and its heart-beat can be easily identified. Two hearts are then beating together in the mother's body; but the small heart depends entirely on the large one, not only for the blood supply which brings it nourishment, but even more for the love which will allow it to develop its full human potential.

12. Any form of abortion, however early it is performed and by whatever expert, is so crude and brutal as hardly to bear description. One method is for the little body to be 'scraped out', that is to say cut up within the womb and pulled out in pieces with a forceps. Alternatively and more often the body is 'sucked out' in parts by vacuum extraction. A third method – though this one tends to be avoided now as carrying risk to the mother – was to replace the fluid in which the baby lives by a salt or glucose solution; this burned up the foetus or killed it slowly by poisoning, and it was born dead some time afterwards by a false labour. At later stages of the pregnancy, the baby is removed from the mother by a surgical operation. When lifted out of its home in the mother's womb, it is still alive. After a while it dies of exposure. People speak of a non-viable baby (one which cannot live outside the womb) as being not yet human. Let us not forget that any one of us would be non-viable if unable to walk and left out for long enough without clothing in the snow.

13. It is not pleasant to speak of these matters. The facts of abortion are ugly. But they are the facts. It is dishonest to conceal them, or to speak of them in impersonal clinical phrases like 'termination of pregnancy', 'scraping the uterine lining', 'emptying the uterus', and so on. Smooth words will not change evil things into good. Killing a baby is still killing a baby even if people call it 'termination of pregnancy', or more smoothly, 'deconception'. For a man to kill his next-door neighbour is still murder, even if the man says he is only 'terminating the occupancy of the adjoining residence'.

14. Abortion does not become in any degree less ugly or less evil if some State law permits it or if it is done in a public hospital by a specialist under a government health service. Mothers who consent to have this done have usually not been allowed to know, or have not permitted themselves to think, about what it is that is being done to their baby. At seminars and discussions promoting abortion, lecturers impress upon nursing personnel that mothers are never in any circumstances to be told what the operation involves, and that the word 'baby' is strictly never to be used in their hearing. It is to be replaced by such impersonal terms as 'fetal parts', 'fetal tissue', 'contents of the uterus', etc. In this same connection, it is significant that research in America has found a high incidence of anxiety and guilt-feeling among para-medical personnel involved in abortions. This is true particularly among nurses. The occurrence of anxiety and guilt-feelings is related to the closeness of involvement in the actual abortion operation. One report states: 'The effect of actual observation and participation in the abortion procedure appears to be a powerful determinant in activating anxiety-producing psychological processes.'

This report goes on to recommend that social workers involved in abortion work be so trained that they can help the other personnel involved to overcome their 'negative emotional reactions'. The technique recommended for doing this is to direct their attention away from the foetus, the operation and its result, and to divert it to the problems of the mother.

15. It should be noted that the lobby which campaigned for legalised abortion in Britain planned their propaganda very carefully and selected their themes very skilfully. They made a deliberate decision to concentrate on the 'hard cases'. The campaign was led by a body called the Abortion Law Reform Association. Two of the members of this body wrote a book about their campaign. One of the things they say is this: 'There was (and still is) so much latent public distaste for the very idea of abortion that it was obvious throughout the Reform Campaign that they would only be able to carry the country with them if they concentrated on the hard cases.'

The same two writers make a number of other revealing statements. They point out that the Association made great play with opinion surveys. They admit that in the area of abortion 'almost all figures were (and still are) subject to dispute'; but they go on to say that the organisers of the campaign discovered that opinion surveys were, as they very candidly put it, a 'match-winning tactic'. Another successful tactic, they report, was to involve the women's organisations in the movement. Every move depended, of course, on the help of the media, and this was willingly forthcoming. Our two authors recorded with delight that 'the mass-circulation newspapers realised that abortion was a popular subject', and that from the moment this realisation dawned, 'every event was eagerly gobbled up and disgorged by press, radio and television'. Finally, and this was the most important point of all, the Association worked hard and successfully at, as they put it, 'lining up friends at the centre of power'. It is useful to bear in mind these hints from inside the movement about how a successful lobby in the area of public morality is worked.

RIGHTS OF THE UNBORN

16. People who support abortion speak as if the unborn baby had no rights. Yet, if a father dies before his child is born, regardless of what the stage of the pregnancy, the child when born has legal rights of inheritance. In the case of the thalidomide babies, babies injured between the time of conception and birth were found entitled to compensation. Recently the English Law Commission recommended that compensation be claimable for unborn babies injured in the womb by the fault of another. The United Nations Organisation in 1959 declared: 'The child, because of its physical and mental immaturity, needs special care and safeguards, including legal safeguards, before as well as after birth.'

Considerable embarrassment is caused to legal people by the effort to reconcile these facts with the law permitting the killing of unborn babies.

17. Recently some philosophers and theologians have argued that the person becomes a person only when recognised as such by the community. They call this an act of 'humanisation'. To refuse birth to a child, they claim, simply means that it is not being accepted or recognised as a person, and that therefore it is not a person. But the point is that we are not free to refuse to recognise another human being as a person. Refusal to recognise another human being as a person is in fact the essence of all immorality in human relations. It is the basis of all oppression, torture, denial of civil rights, religious and racial discrimination, exploitation, all forms of inhumanity of man to man. All of these are simply ways of refusing to recognise other human beings as human. Once human life exists, we are *morally bound* to respect its right to life, to development, to human dignity. Otherwise, the very basis of morality is undermined.

18. The earliest Christian writers had no hesitation in calling abortion murder, no matter at what stage of the pregnancy it was performed. One writer, Tertullian, already in the second century, said:

To prevent birth is anticipated murder; it makes little difference whether one destroys a life already born or does away with it in its nascent stage. The one who is to become a man is already a man.

19. In any case, modern genetic science makes it more difficult to deny that the human soul is present from the moment of conception. As we have pointed out earlier, the embryo, from the first instant, possesses all the genetic characteristics of the adult. The programme for future development is already laid down on the first day of unborn life. The adventure of every human life begins in the womb. The foetus could never become human if it were not human already. The view which is most in har-

mony with modern science is that the spiritual soul is present from the first moment of conception.

CONSEQUENCES OF ABORTION

20. When discussing abortion in the past, people used to speak of the cruel dilemma of 'choice' between the life of the mother, which could be endangered by the continuance of the pregnancy, and the life of her unborn child. Such cases were always extremely few in number. We thank God that nowadays, where modern obstetric facilities are available, such cases are almost non-existent. It is strange that the pressure for abortion should have come principally from those countries where medical science is most advanced; for in fact advances in medicine and progress in ante-natal and obstetric services had eliminated most of the cases in which pregnancy could be a danger to the life of the mother.

21. The statistics from countries which have legalised abortion are revealing in this regard. The 'indications' for which abortion is sought and obtained are for the most part of a psychological, social or economic kind, rather than based on grounds of physical danger or disease. Figures for England show that the 'life or death' situation applied to only a tiny fraction of the total number of abortions. Taken together, all cases that could for any reason, whether medical of psychological, be really called 'hard cases', account for not more than 2 per cent of all the registered abortions carried out in England in recent years.

22. Some abortions are now performed on the grounds of the likelihood of the child's being born defective or handicapped. This, however, even if it could be demonstrated with certainty, would still not justify the deliberate killing of the innocent. It may be hard to see the meaning of a handicapped child's life, and hard for parents to accept it, if they do not look at life on earth with the eyes of faith. But if we judge life and its worth by the standards of physical health and worldly welfare alone, then we have quite simply turned our backs upon the Gospel of Christ. In any case, those who have not experienced it will never know the amount of consolation that has been brought to parents in reward for the stress of caring for their handicapped child. The capacity for affection of many of these children is the joy of their parents' hearts. History will never calculate the amount of good that has been brought into our world by the devotion of parents and the care of the wider community in coping with the problems of handicapped children. Great progress has been made recently in social attitudes to this problem and in social provision for it. Great advances have ben made in the education of children suffering from all forms of handicap. This is one outstanding example of how society can uplift itself by accepting and coping with suffering. Abortion, on the other hand, is a striking instance of how society can degrade and perhaps destroy itself by systematic refusal of suffering.

23. Abortion does not even succeed in eliminating suffering. It has to

be remembered that God has provided in the mother's body quite remarkable systems of security and protection for the unborn child during all the stages of the pregnancy. Interference with these systems can be injurious to the mother as well as fatal to the child. These systems include instincts deeply embedded in the mother's personality. Abortion, by violating these womanly instincts, can lead in the long run to psychological disturbance to the mother. Some researchers have reported a notable proportion of mothers who suffer emotional disturbance after the abortion. Many suffer, in one degree or another, from guilt-feelings. There is a tendency, in much of the discussion about abortions, to ignore such findings. They are likely to be verified particularly, of course, in countries of Christian and especially Catholic background; but similar reports have come from non-Christian countries like Japan. It should be noted too that a high proportion of legal abortions are sanctioned for psychiatric reasons; but it is known that those mothers who are severely emotionally disturbed by a pregnancy are precisely the ones who are more likely to be disturbed by post-abortion doubts and guilt-feelings. Research also suggests that some harmful physical effects for the mother herself and some risks for her future pregnancies can be traced to abortion.

LEGALISATION INCREASES DEMAND

24. Since the Abortion Act came into force in Britain in 1967, the number of abortions notified has risen steadily year by year, going from 25,000 in 1968 to 170,000 in 1973. The figures speak for themselves. As the law stands at present, the situation seems to come very close to abortion on demand. And all this, it should be noted, is happening in a country where there is widespread availability and use of contraceptives. The two pro-abortion writers whom we quoted earlier point out that 'the problem [of unwanted children] is actually getting worse, despite the universal availability of contraceptives.' They argue: 'Abortion on request is a logical concomitant of contraception on demand.'

Availability of contraception will not lessen recourse to abortion: it will only spread still further the mentality and style of life which produce the demand for abortion. There are no easy options to take the place of moral living.

25. Some people sincerely believe that a legal measure of control would at least reduce the number of criminal abortions, with all the appalling risks and problems which these are causing. There are indications, however, that criminal abortions are continuing, side by side with the legal abortions. This has also been the experience in other countries with a longer history than Britain of legalised abortion. Furthermore, abusive practices operating under the actual cover of the law have often gone far to remove the distinction between criminal and legal abortions.

26. A responsible society would surely find other ways of coping with

the problem of criminal abortions than simply to try to introduce legal abortion. Protection for unborn life should be part of society's whole commitment to the improvement of the quality of human life. There is a strange contrast in modern society between the genuine compassion which lies behind movements to abolish capital punishment and to reform the whole penal code for offenders, on the one hand, and, on the other, the barbarous killing of unborn babies. Indeed, the more one thinks of the terrible crime which abortion is, the more one finds that it is in complete contradiction with everything that a caring and compassionate society wishes to be. Modern society sincerely wishes and tries to be caring and compassionate. How can one explain the contradiction? One seems forced to the conclusion that sexual freedom has become such an obsession with modern society that it will sacrifice anything, even unborn babies, to appease this new absolute.

'YES' TO LIFE

27. The Constitution on the Church in the Modern World of Vatican II declared: 'God has conferred on man the surpassing ministry of safeguarding life, a ministry which must be fulfilled in a manner worthy of man. Therefore, from the moment of conception, life must be guarded with the greatest care — abortion and infanticide are unspeakable crimes.'

28. But we should not just say that the Church is 'against abortion'. We should say that the Church is for life. The Church says 'Yes' to life. The Church has been saying 'Yes' to unborn life, without any hesitation or reservation, for two thousand years. In recent years, since the abortion debate became a public issue in country after country, nearly every Catholic Hierarchy in Europe, in America and everywhere the issue has been raised, has responded by once more clearly and strongly and unanimously repeating this great 'Yes' to unborn life.

29. In Ireland, we are far from being unaffected by the problem and by the accompanying discussion. Experience elsewhere, as we have already indicated, shows only too clearly what carefully organised pressure-groups can do to confuse and then to change public opinion. More immediately disturbing is the fact that considerable numbers of Irish girls are already going to England each year to have abortions performed. At present more than 2,200 Irish girls are officially registered as having abortions in Britain each year. More than half of these are from the Republic. Since the introduction of legal abortion, probably at least 8,000 Irish-resident girls and women have had abortions under the British Act. Over half of these are from the Republic. This clearly could not be happening without encouragement and advice from people they consult in this country. Those who advise or arrange abortions for girls and women who consult them bear as great, if not a greater degree of guilt than the girls and

women themselves. These figures indicate widespread moral confusion and lack of knowledge. This is the context in which we write this Letter.

30. As we write it, we are aware of the agonies of conscience and the tortures of remorse which many girls who have had abortions are now suffering. We want to speak to them too. We want to assure them of the boundless compassion and unlimited mercy of Christ. He loves them. He loves to forgive. He has told us that he has more joy in forgiving sinners than he receives from the just who do not think they need forgiveness. No-one is excluded from his love. No matter what the past, he offers everyone forgiveness and peace. His 'Yes' to life is also an unconditional 'Yes' to all who come in sorrow and love to ask his pardon

THE QUALITY OF LIFE

31. The Church says 'Yes', not just to human existence, but to the quality and dignity of human life. The Christian demand is that all human life should be permitted and enabled to develop to the full dignity and quality of living which befit a human person and child of God. Nothing less than that is what is commanded by Christ's command to love our neighbour as we love our own self. The Christian 'Yes' to life includes a call for freedom, for adequate education, for proper living conditions, for more just distribution of wealth and opportunity, for protection of the human environment, and for more responsible use of the resources of nature. The Church is not simply 'against abortion'; she is *for* life and *for* man and for human dignity and social justice.

32. It is often said nowadays that we should not consider so much the mere existence of life, but rather the quality which that life has the prospect of attaining. Some argue that unless unborn life can be assured of a certain quality, then the mere fact of its existence is deprived of value. Or that if the existence of unborn life seriously lessens the prospect of an acceptable quality of life for the mother or her family, then the unborn life cannot be said to have a right to exist.

33. This argument turns moral principles upside down. Life has the right to quality and dignity because it exists. Life does not derive the right to exist from the quality which circumstances seem likely to give to it. Once human life exists, then those who conceived it have the obligation to respect its right to continue to exist. They have, at the same time, the obligation to create the conditions which will enable it to develop in a manner worthy of its human dignity. If parents cannot themselves ensure this, then society has the strict duty to come to their help with all the supports that are necessary to give this new life a quality corresponding to its sacred character as a human person, made in the image of God.

Abortion and the Right to Life

ARCHBISHOPS OF GREAT BRITAIN

1. We, the Catholic archbishops of Great Britain, address this joint statement on abortion to our fellow Christians and indeed to our fellow-citizens of every religion and none.

2. We speak in defence of life against the evil of abortion. We speak in a society where all enjoy a freedom which is rightly prized and which was affirmed by the Catholic Church in the second Vatican Council; a full freedom of religious belief and practice, and a freedom to seek the truth about everything including moral matters. We live in a society where many differing moral and political opinions are conscientiously held and pursued in practice. We make no attempt to override the consciences of our fellow-citizens. We do not seek to have all Catholic moral teaching imposed by law, or even adopted as public policy.

3. But we too have the right, as members of this pluralistic society, to appeal to the consciences not only of our fellow-Catholics, but also of our fellow-citizens and our political leaders and representatives. We too have consciences. And we cannot in conscience remain silent while the most basic human beings are ignored and over-ridden by the law and, increasingly, by the public policies and everyday practices of our country. These developing human lives may be unborn and silent but they are already our neighbours, living in our midst and are part of our human family. They need to be defended.

AN ISSUE OF BASIC HUMAN RIGHTS AND DIGNITY

4. The Church speaks out against abortion, as it has from the beginning, because it acknowledges the human rights and dignity of all, including the unborn, and is committed to their defence. There is here a crucial point of principle. It has everything to do with the intrinsic value and inalienable rights of each individual. It is a matter of respect for our neighbour.

5. Our stand against abortion is one aspect of our stand against all practices that degrade human rights and dignity. Scottish bishops have made many statements, both individually and collectively, on the need to aid developing nations, on social justice at home and abroad, on unemployment problems and on help for the needy and deprived. The bishops of England and Wales issued in 1971 a major statement on moral questions which ranged over Christian living, race relations, violence and

peace. Since then the bishops have tackled the housing problem, disarmament and many current social issues. The bishops have tried to defend the insulted, the despised, the disadvantaged. With other Christians we have resisted racism. We have stressed the brotherhood of man and rejected any discrimination based on colour or race.

6. The whole of Christian social teaching can be seen as an appeal to the conscience of the relatively well-off and powerful to give practical recognition to the humanity and rights of the poor and the weak. And that social teaching proclaims as well the rights of minorities against majorities who treat them with unfair indifference or hostility.

7. More often than not the expected child is wanted and welcomed by parents and family and is later received without question by the community at large. But when we look at the law of our land, when we reflect on the practices which result in over 140,000 registered abortions a year, when we note the changing attitudes of many who work in health care, we feel obliged to say: unborn children in Great Britain are today a legally disadvantaged class; they are weak; they are a minority. So they are entitled to be defended by anyone of humane conscience, but also, particularly, by those who, like us, profess that every human being without exception has the unique dignity of an eternal destiny.

PROTECTING THE INNOCENT AGAINST DIRECT ATTACKS

8. What we have to say about abortion is consistent with the whole Christian teaching about the right of the innocent to live. That teaching is central to our civilisation. Without it, no other human rights are secure. Sometimes there are occasions when individuals or nations, in self-defence, may rightly use force, even deadly force, against anyone who by his own use of a similar degree of force is unjustly attacking them. But the right of self-defence is limited; it never entitles us directly to kill the innocent, that is those who are not contributing to the unjust attack.

9. This is why the second Vatican Council emphatically declared that every warlike act directed to the indiscriminate destruction of whole cities or large areas with their inhabitants is a crime. The reason for that teaching is that any such act, because indiscriminate, would inevitably involve a direct attack on the life of innocent inhabitants of these cities or other areas.

10. The Catholic teaching on abortion is no more than one application of the fundamental teaching that the innocent may not be directly attacked.

EACH OF THE UNBORN IS A UNIQUE, HUMAN INDIVIDUAL

11. Even before the processes of human reproduction became well understood, Christian teaching always regarded the unborn, at all stages of pregnancy, as possessed of a distinct, new life which no one could rightly

seek to destroy. For many centuries, Christians like others took for granted scientific and philosophical theories which suggested that the newly-conceived human being did not become formed or ensouled until several weeks after conception. So in those times the ecclesiastical penalties and censures for causing an abortion early in a pregnancy were often less severe than those for abortion in later pregnancy. But throughout those centuries, the Church never wavered in its teaching that abortion, at whatever stage of pregnancy, is seriously wrongful. Today the course of human development is much better understood. Modern science enables us to see better than ever before the fundamental significance of the time of conception.

12. For at the time of conception there comes into existence a new life. There is a union in which a living cell from the father fertilises a living cell from the mother. That union, a transmission of life, is the beginning of new life. Usually this new life is and will always remain a single individual; sometimes, in ways not fully understood, there may then or a few days later be division resulting, for example, in identical twins. But scientists can tell us that, from the time of conception, the features which distinguish us from each of our parents—the colour of our eyes, our shape of face, and so on—are all laid down in the 'genetic code' that comes into existence then. Each such new life is the life not of a potential human being but of a human being with potential. The development of this potential is normally a process of profound continuity. No one can point to, say, the fourth week of that process, or the eighth, the twelfth, the twentieth, the twenty-fourth or twenty-eighth, and say: 'That is when I began being me'. Birth itself is certainly an event in the life-story of each one of us. But for the beginning of that story we must look to the time of our conception.

13. The unborn child has not yet developed all its potentialities, and it is dependent on its mother. But the newly born infant too is dependent and even adults have not yet developed all their potentialities. Scientists can tell us more and more details of the ways in which the bodily organisation of the growing child in the womb is, from the beginning, biologically distinct and clearly separate from the pregnant woman's body, which is physically contributing to, sustaining and embracing her child's. It makes nonsense to speak of this living and developing being as simply a part of the woman's body. Medical technology can reveal to us the early stages of the child's heartbeat, brainwaves, muscular movement, sensitivity to touch—all within a few weeks of conception. We believe that all this is becoming more and more widely known. Certainly it deserves to be known, for the development and essential completion of the bodily constitution of the child in the womb is one of the wonders of this created universe. And this knowledge helps to break down the prejudice that the human community consists of those already born or viable. That prejudice is the root of the newly respectable yet still unjust discrimination

which is abortion.

ABORTION IS UNFAIR DISCRIMINATION

14. Much is made in society today of woman's rights and within the abortion debate much is made of a woman's rights over her own body. No doubt we all have certain moral rights but, of course, no rights are unlimited. The question of a woman's rights in respect of her own body is too often put as a one-sided slogan which is deceptive and which ignored consideration for others and for the bodily rights of others. Many responsibilities arise from the need to respect the rights of others.

15. Since men and women have rights in respect of their own bodies, children have such rights too. It does not matter whether we call our children 'neonates' (the medical term for those just born), or 'fetuses' (the medical term for the unborn in mid or late-pregnancy), or 'embryos' (a medical term for the unborn in all earlier stages of pregnancy); the fact remains that the young and growing offspring of human parents are children. Unborn children have rights in respect of their own bodies, even while they are enclosed within and sustained by their mothers' bodies.

16. What is their right? It is the right not to be made the object of attack. So the course of their development before birth must not be interfered with by any procedure or technical process carried out with the intention of preventing the continuation of that development. When we speak of abortion and condemn any attempt to procure it, we are referring to any procedure or technique which is adopted with that intention. Interference with the unborn child just in order to get rid of it would obviously be abortion, even if one did not positively want to kill it but acted regardless of the certainty or risk that it would thereby die. If a technique or device achieves such effects after conception, it is in fact an abortifacient, an abortion-device, even if it is often called by other names, such as 'contraceptive' or 'menstrual extraction' and so on.

17. Some abortions, perhaps many, appear to be performed for reasons which are basically selfish or even trivial. Others are the results of strong social and psychological pressure. Lack of support, or even hostility, from the father of the child, especially if the pregnancy is seen as a failure in the use of contraception, may leave the mother abandoned and despairing. A similar attitude of recrimination from parents or friends can drive a lonely unmarried girl to a final decision which in her heart she does not really want. In many such cases it is difficult to think of abortion as in any full sense a free choice on the part of the mother against her defenceless unborn child and also against her deeper instincts of preservation and love for her offspring. Honest recognition by others of their duties and responsibilities towards the pregnant woman and her child would often remove the pressures driving towards abortion.

JUSTICE FOR THE UNBORN

18. Termination of pregnancy by induced abortion means death for the unborn. It means killing. That is what is offered as the solution to problems of inconvenience or embarrassment, or of some risk to the mental or physical well-being of the mother or perhaps of her other children. To condemn such a solution as we do is not to minimise those problems. But we cannot shirk the fact that bringing up children after their birth can likewise cause problems of inconvenience, embarrassment, poverty and risk to their parents and brothers and sisters. The 'moral' arguments for abortion can equally be used as arguments for infanticide, for killing children after birth. That is the logic which the pagan world before Christ followed to its conclusion; the 'exposure' that is killing by act or neglect of unwanted or inconvenient children after birth. It has to be recognised that neither birth, nor viability, makes any real difference to the intrinsic rights of a human being. Our civilisation still makes a moral judgment about our responsibilities to young children after birth. We all say that they are entitled to care and rescue even at the cost of hard and thankless work or even risk. The same judgment has to be made about our responsibilities to those other children still unborn but who differ only in the degree of their development.

19. These considerations of justice are real and valid. We realise that to many people they will seem hard and unfeeling. The pregnant girl or woman experiences her situation with all its difficulties and may see her unborn child as a threat rather than as a living human being. Those among whom she lives are aware of her present problems which may cry out for practical measures of relief and support. The unborn child, on the other hand, remains unseen and unheard, with a life and destiny which only the future can bring to light. It takes a vigorous effort of imagination and of clear, 'hard' thinking to appreciate that the unborn child has a claim which cannot be outweighed by inconveniences and risks and a life which cannot fairly be sacrificed for reasons of health; the unborn child has a claim which calls for the respect due to a living human being.

THE HANDICAPPED ARE ENTITLED TO LIVE

20. But what about a child who will or may be born handicapped in mind or body? Here again we must be clear. No one has a right to kill another human on the basis that that other would be 'better off dead'. Once we see that the child before birth is not essentially different from the child after birth, we are also forced to conclude that selective abortion, that is killing unborn children to save them from a life of handicap, is also to be condemned. Such selective abortions are equivalent to asserting the essential rightness of euthanasia—the killing of the aged, infirm or handicapped, with or without their consent, because someone judges that they would be better off dead. And these abortions are profoundly at

odds with the caring work for handicapped children and adults to which so many of our fellow-Christians and fellow-citizens have devoted and are devoting so much of their lives. Many handicapped people are themselves deeply opposed to abortion, having discovered for themselves the inner richness of human existence.

PARTICULARLY HARD CASES

21. *Rape.* We speak with equal feeling about the bodily rights of women and of their unborn, perhaps unwanted offspring. People sometimes argue that abortions are justified if a child is conceived as a consequence of rape. Who can adequately express the outrage suffered by the victim of a rape? A woman is certainly entitled to defend herself against the continuing effects of such an attack and to seek immediate medical assistance with a view to preventing conception. In a very small number of cases, conception may in fact occur. Then there exists a new being whose individuality, distinct from each of its parents and from any of their cells, we have already described. From that time, the requirements of the moral law, transcending even the most understandable emotional reactions, are clear; the newly conceived child cannot rightly be made to suffer the penalty of death for a man's violation of the woman.

22. *Danger of death of the mother.* Catholic teaching on abortion accords fully with principles of moral reasonableness. The abortion that must be judged always unacceptable to the upright moral conscience is the direct abortion that we described earlier (para 16); those procedures and techniques that are intended to stop the unborn child's continuing development. We are not speaking of cases where the interference with the unborn child is in fact an unintended, though foreseen, side-effect of procedures necessary to save the mother from some underlying or supervening condition that threatens her life. For example, a treatment for cancer of the uterus can be justified even if it also causes a miscarriage. Even in such cases, however, it is the doctor's duty to regard both the mother and the unborn child as his patients, and to try to sustain the pregnancy so long as there is any reasonable prospect of saving both of them.

23. If there remain any cases, which in contemporary medicine are certainly exceedingly rare or perhaps even non-existent, in which the life of the mother could not be saved without a direct abortion, a sensitive and upright conscience must in these cases be guided by the fundamental principles which govern all these matters; innocent life is not to be directly attacked; the unborn child has an intrinsic right to life.

24. In such a situation, the law of God, which is also the rule of reason, makes exceptionally high demands. In reaffirming that law we are not asserting that the law of the land should treat as criminal the acts of someone who, in that situation, does not acknowledge or does not live up to those demands. But we point out, once again, that what we have to say

about abortion is but one application of wider principles. The principles that the Church proclaims are not for some ideal or theoretical world or for humanity in the abstract. They speak directly to the consciences of men and women in this world. They are principles that can on occasion demand heroic self-sacrifice of individuals and nations. For there are situations, for example in war, in which self-defence could not be effective without the commission of acts which must never be done, whatever the consequences. Innocent hostages, for example, must never be killed. And having said all that, we may add that the truly practical and pressing problem in modern Britain is not the tiny proportion of cases in which the mother's life is in jeopardy. The real problem is rather this. The vast majority of abortions carried out in Great Britain represent a massive and growing trivialisation of human life, an increasing acceptance of the practice of killing on demand.

LAW AND PRACTICE IN BRITAIN

25. *The law of the land.* We have said (para 2) that the Catholic Church does not ask that the law of the land should coincide in every respect with the moral law. And, in relation to abortion, we have just mentioned (para 24) a situation in which the requirements of the criminal law might reasonably be less demanding than those of a truly moral conscience. As Catholic archbishops of Great Britain we do not intend now to make a complete commentary on either the present or the ideal state of the law on abortion. But we will say three things:

1. Law ought to uphold and embody the principles that are basic to our civilisation and our existing law in every other field; innocent life is to be protected by the criminal law and public policy; no law should countenance discrimination by the strong against the weak.
2. The present law, the Abortion Act 1967, is grossly unjust. It permits the killing of the unborn because of some 'substantial risk' that they may suffer some 'serious handicap'. It wrongly presumes that such people can be treated as if they were 'better off dead'.
3. The Abortion Act's criterion for lawful abortion is essentially the same criterion as any doctor would use in any operation when only one patient is at stake: 'Will operating involve greater risks than not operating?' Thus, apart from some extra paperwork, our law seems to put abortion on a par with cosmetic operations. It treats the presence of a new human being as insignificant. It treats the very life and existence of that new human being as out-weighed in value by another human being's perhaps slight or passing problems of physical or mental well-being.

In these ways, the Abortion Act 1967 departs fundamentally from the most basic tradition of our law: the innocent and weak, as much as the powerful and healthy, are entitled to the equal protection of the law.

26. *Conscience and medical practice.* Having spoken about the existing law as it affects the unborn and those who have to deal with them, we must say something about the way this law is tending in practice to affect medical personnel because of their conscientiously held beliefs about the rights of the innocent to live. It is hard to deny that there are talented and devoted men and women who are, in effect, being debarred, or at least seriously deterred, from pursuing their chosen speciality, not only in obstetrics and gynaecology but in other medical spheres closely related to the abortion procedure. Simple reform of the conscientious-objection clauses of the Abortion Act 1967 would not be enough to put an end to this deplorable development. Positive administrative action should be instituted both in hospitals and the community services to ensure that the many thousands already engaged are not indirectly induced to act in conflict with their deepest convictions. Employing authorities should not require participation in the abortion procedure as a necessary condition of employment.

POSIITIVE RESPONSIBILITIES OF CHRISTIANS AND OF SOCIETY

27. A stand against abortion is a stand for humanity. It therefore involves a stand for women, particularly those who are or who may be pregnant. Whether or not her pregnancy results from her inadequate awareness of the moral significance of sexual intercourse, a girl or woman should always be given the practical help she may need to carry through her pregnancy. She should be given it unstintingly and without moral censure. The help may include counselling and advice, for example about the possible adoption of her baby, or about bringing up a one-parent family. But it must always be given in a way that fully respects her freedom and responsibility.

28. Very necessary and very encouraging are the efforts of those voluntary associations in which Catholics and non-Catholics work together to attack abortion at its root by providing moral and material support to any and every mother-to-be who is willing to allow her baby to be born and not aborted. Many of our own dioceses have pledged themselves to provide such help, confidentially and at no expense to the woman; this help includes, if she wishes, the care for her baby after birth. But more, much more, will need to be done, by Catholics and by all who care about mother and child alike. Governments and local authorities, too, are not entitled to look to abortion to relieve them from their responsibilities, for example to tackle the problems caused by shortage of housing. Still less may they treat abortion as a 'solution' to problems of overcrowded schooling, one-parent families, and juvenile delinquency. Calculations of cost-effectiveness and drives for economy must always be subordinate to basic principles of human rights.

A WORD OF ENCOURAGEMENT

29. To all who are working *against* abortion and *for* the life and future of the unborn and their distressed mothers, we say: do not be discouraged. The laws, practices and opinions of our society may seem, at times, all too firmly set in favour of abortion. Substantial reform may at times seem beyond reach—let alone the full justice which you seek. But your work is not in vain. At the very least it preserves our society from greater and more rapid corruption. At the very least it also preserves for everyone an option that would otherwise become stifled and forgotten; the option—of pregnant women and their relatives and friends, of doctors, of nurses, of social workers —to respect innocent life and to refuse to take part in its destruction. And at best, your efforts may well be crowned with success. Success has so often appeared to social reformers to be beyond their reach, almost up to the moment when they attained it.

A CALL TO COMMITMENT

30. By practising and condoning abortion, our society has lost its way. Each one of us must ask what we have done and are doing to help show the way to those of our fellow-citizens who have lost their bearings in this matter. If we are in medical practice, nursing or social work, have we really stood firm? If we are teachers, have we taught without compromise? If we are young and eager for justice, have we extended our concern to our neighbours, the unborn? Very many of us must now recognise that we have not done enough. Now is the time for those of goodwill to commit themselves, in one way or another, to work *against* abortion and *for* the life and future of the unborn and their distressed mothers.

31. To our fellow-Catholics we can add this: when we acknowledge and respect the sanctity ol human life we are acknowledging both the unique value of every human individual made in the image and likeness of God, and the domination of God over that life and over its creation and its ending. Work against abortion and for the life of the unborn and their distressed mothers is a work of true charity, of everlasting significance. As Pope John Paul II, in his first encyclical, *Redemptor hominis,* recalls (para 16), we must all be mindful of the scene of the last judgment according to the words of Christ related to Matthew's Gospel (Matt 25:31-46). Going beyond those words to their wider meaning, we must suppose that when that day of judgment comes, the Lord will confront those who without justice, mercy or repentance killed the innocent unborn. But he will also address those who tried to save the lives of those innocents. And to them, we may surely suppose, the Lord will say: 'Inasmuch as you defended the least of these, you defended me'.

The Sacredness of Human Life

IRISH CATHOLIC BISHOPS' CONFERENCE*

1. A crisis has arisen concerning abortion in Ireland. The bishops share the widespread dismay at the recent Supreme Court judgement which envisages legal abortion in the Republic of Ireland. The understanding of the Irish people was that the right to life of the unborn was protected by the Constitution in such a way as to render abortion illegal. Abortion has now been declared to be legal. The consequences are from every point of view extremely grave.

2. Human life is a gift from God. 'For it was you who created my being, knit me together in my mother's womb. I thank you for the wonder of my being, for the wonders of all creation' (Ps 139).

3. From the moment a human life begins to exist at conception it is entitled to the same respect and protection as any other human life. Any action which sets out to destroy this life is morally wrong. The lives of both the child and the mother are sacred. The right to life of each of them is inviolable. Abortion is the direct taking of innocent life and no motive can justify it. No court judgement, no act of legislation, can make it morally right. Abortion goes to the very wellsprings of human life and touches the very foundations of morality.

4. As bishops we are servants of Christ's truth; we are also servants of his love. We understand the anguish and distress of pregnant women in difficult situations who might wrongly feel that abortion is the only solution open to them. We know the trauma which women suffer before an abortion and from which they may continue to suffer long afterwards. The Church always seeks to offer the mercy, healing and forgiveness of Christ. The Church in Ireland is committed to providing all forms of support and care through Cura and similar organisations throughout the country.

5. It now appears that our laws and our courts do not give to the the unborn child the protect to which he or she has a right. This poses an inescapable challenge to the whole of our society and this challenge must be faced without delay.

6. As bishops we have a duty to proclaim the Gospel to our people. We also have a duty to make our contribution to building a society which reflects the dignity of human beings in the light of the Gospel. The issue of abortion is an matter of justice. It involves the most basic of all human

* Statement issued after meeting of 9 to 11 March 1992.

rights, the right to life. It must therefore be a matter of serious concern to the whole of society. The protection of human rights, including the rights of the unborn, is a moral imperative for every society.

7. Whenever abortion has been legalised, there is continual agitation to alter the legislation, whether to make it more restrictive or to remove the restrictions. Experience has shown that laws permitting abortion even in restricted circumstances rapidly lead to abortion on demand.

8. A particularly urgent challenge now faces our legislators as they seek to exercise their responsibility to protect the lives of unborn children, who are the weakest and most voiceless members of our human family. The matter is of the utmost importance and must be addressed without delay. Legislators need and deserve the support of every citizen in discharging this fundamental responsibility.

9. God is the author of all human life. We must implore his Holy Spirit that the overriding concern of all of us at this time will be absolute respect for the sacredness of the life which comes from him.

Reaction to the Supreme Court Judgement

STANDING COMMITTEE OF THE GENERAL SYNOD OF THE CHURCH OF IRELAND*

In June 1982 the Standing Committee of the General Synod sent the following official comment on behalf of the Church of Ireland to the Taoiseach, Mr Haughey:

> We cannot emphasise too strongly the right to life and this includes the right of the yet unborn. The Lambeth Conference of 1958 received a Committee Report in which it was stated:
>
>> In the strongest terms, Christians reject the practice of induced abortion, or infanticide, which involves the killing of a life already conceived (as well as a violation of the personality of the mother) save at the dictate of strict and undeniable medical necessity.
>
> This implies clearly that there can be medical circumstances in which a termination of pregnancy is required.

*Statement issued 2 April 1992

In our opinion a proposed amendment to the Constitution and a referendum will not alter the human situation as it exists in the country, contribute to its amelioration or promote a responsible and informed attitude to the issue of abortion. We gravely doubt the wisdom of using constitutional prohibitions as a means of dealing with complex moral and social problems.

This view was reiterated in a Statement issued on behalf of the Standing Committee in March 1983 and in a further Statement issued by the Archbishops of Armagh and Dublin in August 1983.

The Standing Committee at its meeting [in March 1992] took note of the decision of the Supreme Court in the case of *Attorney General v. X*, and in particular that the four learned judges who comprised the majority applied the test of 'real and substantial risk' to the life of the mother. This test corresponds closely with that of 'strict and undeniable medical necessity', and is therefore to be welcomed.

The Standing Committee appreciates the nature and complexity of the problems to which the Government in now seeking solutions. The Committee believes that, while the Church of Ireland is but one of a number of religious denominations in the State, and while it respects the right of others to make their views known, these official comments made on behalf of the Church of Ireland should receive serious consideration. Against that background, we affirm our previously expressed opinion that the Constitution is an inappropriate instrument for solving complex moral and social problems.

In the circumstances which have now arisen, the Standing Committee urges that provision be made for:

1. A means of determining whether a 'real and substantial risk' to the life of the mother exists.
2. Fixing a stage in pregnancy beyond which its termination would be absolutely prohibited.
3. Information and counselling services as recommended by the Commission on the Status of Women.

The Standing Committee also considers that freedom to leave the State should not restricted except for those who are serving a term of imprisonment or where it is made a condition of bail for those whoa re on remand. In the case of minors, parental consent should be required.

The making of information concerning methods of contraception more widely available and reasonable access to means of contraception are matters not entirely unrelated to the present difficulties. It is now almost six months since the Standing Committee forwarded its comments to the Health (Family Planning) (Amendment) Bill 1991 to the Minister for Health (Dr O'Hanlon), during which period the Bill has not made any progress through the Oireachtas. This should not be further postponed.

Dynamics of Spiritual Living

Course Director: Miceal O'Regan, O.P.

This course is designed for priests and religious who wish to explore the dynamics of their spiritual life in a reflective and meditative context.

Using insights of transpersonal psychology within the Christian tradition, questions such as 'How do we experience the dynamics of our spirit as distinct from the Holy Spirit' (Rom 8:16) and 'How do we experience the emergence of our inner self or hidden man' (Eph 3:16) will be explored.

Venue: Eckhart House, 19 Clyde Road, Dublin 4

Dates: July 10 to 17 and August 7 to 14 1992 (Non-residential)

Apply to: Secretary, Eckhart House. Tel. 01-684687

New from *veritas*
Sharing God's Word

BLESS THIS HOUSE
BRIAN MAGEE CM (ED)

The blessing of a home is a memorable event in the life of a Christian family. Relatives and friends gather to celebrate. Sometimes, however, the actual blessing can take second place to the festivities.

Bless This House provides a ceremony which fits the solemnity of the occasion and encourages the active participation of the family and those present.

It can also be adapted for use on other family occasions such as wedding anniversaries and birthdays and it is designed in a convenient pocket-sized format.

£1.95

7/8 Lower Abbey Street, Dublin 1 Tel: (01) 788177 Fax: (01) 744913
Also: Stillorgan, Cork, Ennis, Sligo, Letterkenny and Dundalk

In DOCTRINE & LIFE in 1992

The Search for God in the Work of the Artist

The Need for a God: Spiritual Quest in the Novels of Brian Moore
JO O'DONOGHUE, author of *Brian Moore: A Critical Study*

The Tragic God of Patrick Kavanagh's 'Great Hunger'
MICHAEL HOWLETT, theologian and literary critic

The Mysticism of T.S. Eliot
ROWAN WILLIAMS, professor of theology at Oxford

The Mystical Journey of the French Priest-novelist Jean Sulivan
PATRICK GORMALLY, professor of romance languages, University College, Galway

Spirituality and the Visual Artist
HILARY PYLE, critic and historian

Plus other series of articles

The Gospel in the New Europe
Reports from the member countries of the Community

The Education Debate
Among the contributors are MARGARET WALSH, past president of ASTI, DERMOT LANE of Mater Dei, and GERRY WHYTE, lecturer in law at TCD.

Millennium Questions
Topics being covered include: 'The Believing Environment at the End of the Decade'; 'The Blinding Effects of False Gods'; 'The Heart of Worship' – all discussed in a way that will encourage dialogue with the readers.

Also from Dominican Publications

religious life review

Edited by Austin Flannery, O.P., and appearing six times a year, *religious life review* concentrates on questions concerning religious life or topics which, though of general interest, are best considered within the context of religious life.

Special interests for 1992

After Persecution: Religious Life in Eastern Europe

Ministry and Renewal

Social Justice in Post-Marxist Times

The Sick and the Elderly

Problems Facing Women Religious

Subscription rates and sample copy available from
Dominican Publications

Also from Dominican Publications

Scripture in Church

120 pages   4 times a year

A guide to understanding the Scripture readings at Mass. For each Sunday and Holy Day there is a Celebrant's Guide plus Biblical Commentary and Homily Notes. Also a Guide for Readers, Reflections for Weekdays and Saints' Days, and useful essays on biblical and liturgical topics.
The editorial team includes Wilfrid Harrington, Michael Maher, Mary Fennell, and Martin McNamara.

Subscription rates and sample copy available from

Dominican Publications
42 PARNELL SQUARE · DUBLIN 1